THERE WAS A FIRE HERE

THERE
WAS A
FIRE HERE

A Memoir

by

RISA NYE

SHE WRITES PRESS

Published 2016
Printed in the United States of America
ISBN: 978-1-63152-045-7
Library of Congress Control Number: 2015956813

For information, address:
She Writes Press
1563 Solano Ave #546
Berkeley, CA 94707

Book design by Stacey Aaronson

She Writes Press is a division of SparkPoint Studio, LLC.

Names and identifying characteristics have been changed to protect the privacy of certain individuals.

For my family

CONTENTS

PART 3

———————

NOTHING

To have nothing. And I mean nothing except the clothes you ran out of the house wearing when you left—when you left before the place burned, before you knew whether you'd be able to go back. Let's say you didn't take much. Let's say what you are left with is nothing.

What are the things you'd miss most? Have you ever asked yourself: if my house were on fire, what would I grab? People ask themselves this question, and they may even come up with a pretty good answer. But the real test is when the fire is raging, and your kids are scared and you don't really know if it's a drill or not. So you play it safe and take some important things, but leave others behind, things that you will torture yourself about later on. But your heart is pounding and you can't think straight because smoke and ashes are in the air, and you have kids and you have to get them and yourself the hell out of there before it's too late.

I remember exactly what I took with me. It wasn't much. A leather jacket, a jewelry box, photograph albums, and baby books.

Decisions made on the fly.

This and not that.

But here's something I hadn't counted on, a consequence of nothing: the freedom, the lightness. To have nothing means no baggage, no decisions, no choices.

There is a moment when a trapeze artist flies from one trapeze to another, maybe reaching for a partner's outstretched hands. It's hang time, a moment when it's just you and gravity, when you are suspended between the thing you left and the thing you are reaching for. And I've heard that particular space and time described as though it were something to be savored and contemplated, even enjoyed, for the sheer excitement of being neither here nor there. Only in between.

I remember that surprising feeling of freedom. Freedom from having. Could anyone else understand this hard-to-explain lightness? And did I ever say this out loud to anyone? No, not in twenty-five years. Only now, as I look back and remember that secret sense of lightness, am I ready to address it.

It was easy to move around without a lot stuff weighing us down. I am speaking now from the perspective of a person who had things, old familiar things, and a nice life. But for a while, I could not fill a shopping cart with what I had left. I would not have wanted to. And that was fine for a long time.

Now, twenty-five years after the fire, my house is full again.

I find myself missing that sense of lightness, that freedom from possessions, and this is a feeling I did not have before the fire. I long for that lightness but do not long for the sense of loss.

And I wonder, is it possible to have one without the other?

PART 1

T H E   B L U E   H O U S E

I n February 1984 our family of four moved into our boxy blue house in the Oakland Hills. After years of living in rentals, my husband Bruce and I were happy to be first-time homeowners. Granted, the house had a few drawbacks. A marble could roll from one corner to the other in our bedroom. The carpet on the stairs resembled old banana bread, and the rooms were painted or papered in wildly competing color schemes. Our bedroom, for example, looked like the inside of a ripe cantaloupe, with jack-o'-lantern orange trim. One wall in our son Myles's deep-blue bedroom sported lively Noah's ark wallpaper, while the room our daughter Caitlin chose featured an eye-crossing plaid. Shortly after we settled in, we discovered that the hot and cold indicators on all the faucets were reversed. It took a couple of bracing showers to figure that one out. Nevertheless, the house was in a great location—across the street from the kids' elementary school.

And every February clusters of yellow daffodils bloomed in the red brick planters out front.

When we moved into the house, Caitlin was in kindergarten and Myles was still in preschool. As far as Bruce and I were concerned, our family was complete: a girl and a boy, almost three years apart. In the house on Hermosa, unlike the previous rental we'd lived in for four years, the kids had their own rooms, and their own bathroom. This was our first purchased house—and we felt the same terror and exuberance that I imagine most first-time buyers feel when they sign that imposing stack of papers.

By the time we bought the house on Hermosa, we'd lived in four rental houses over the course of the nearly twelve years we'd been married. Not that many moves, really. And we never got farther than San Jose, fifty miles from where we went to high school. We moved there in December 1977, when I was nearly nine months pregnant with Caitlin, because of Bruce's first job as a newly minted lawyer. We were about an hour from what we still thought of as home—the East Bay.

Living that far away from friends and family turned out to be a mixed blessing. We were happy to strike out on our own and start our family in a new city, but we didn't anticipate needing the support of the ones we'd left behind. How could we have known that our lives would be turned upside down after the baby arrived?

Immediately following her birth in San Francisco, we discovered that our newborn daughter would require corrective heart surgery, which resulted in her months-long hospitalization and my daily commute to the University of California hospital to sit by her bedside. We nearly lost her when she developed postoperative complications at a time when she was least able to rally. Repeated surgeries left her with scars on her chest, her back, her ankles, and her wrists. To accommodate the IVs they placed on her scalp, she briefly sported a Mohawk. During those trying days, we operated in crisis mode: not sleeping, on edge, in denial, eating badly, suffering from short-term memory loss, with thoughts ping-ponging through our minds at warp speed.

When Caitlin finally came home, she was four and a half months old. She was sleeping through the night, but had to adjust to a room without the bright lights and beeping equipment she was used to in the hospital.

During the time Caitlin was hospitalized, one of the social workers at UCSF asked me if I'd be willing to talk to other parents who had babies in the Intensive Care Nursery—parents of kids with heart disease, in particular. I agreed, and enjoyed doing it, but felt as though I could benefit from some background and training, not just relying on my own experience. In 1982, I decided to go back to school and get a degree in counseling. So I took a graduate entrance exam and applied to the closest California State University campus, in Hayward. I passed my exam with colors that didn't necessarily fly, but were good enough for me to gain acceptance to the counseling program. That fall, I took the kids to the student daycare center and raced up the hill to my morning classes. When class was over, I raced back down the hill, picked up the kids, had Caitlin eat her lunch in the car (if I remembered to pack her one—otherwise it was a juice box, peanut butter crackers, and a banana from the local 7-Eleven), and got her home in time for her to walk to kindergarten with a neighbor girl. When she'd started school in the fall, Myles and I walked her to the corner and saw her cross the street safely. He dearly missed his older sister and playmate for the half day she was in school.

THE HOUSE ON HERMOSA HAD BEEN OWNED BY ONE OF Caitlin's kindergarten classmate's parents. One day on the playground, the mother of this little boy casually mentioned that they would be moving and putting their house on the market. Bruce and I had recently started talking about buying a house, and had looked at a few in the neighborhood. "Where is your house?" I asked her.

She pointed to the square blue house directly across from the schoolyard. The red brick planters were full of bright-yellow daffodils. "Would you like to look at it?" she asked. "We're having an open house this weekend."

"You live across the street from school?" It seemed too good to be true. I told her yes, we would certainly look at her house.

We asked our more experienced next-door neighbors, who had bought and sold five or six houses already, to come with us and help us evaluate the situation. We had no idea what to look for or what kinds of questions to ask. The four of us walked through the rooms, looked in the backyard, peeked in the garage, and sized up the closets. Once our inspection was complete, we walked down the steps to the sidewalk.

"Well?" I asked. "Think we should make an offer?"

They thought it was a good house for us—big enough, and

the location was hard to beat. So we went ahead and made an appointment with their real estate agent. The next thing we knew, we'd made an offer and it was accepted. I don't normally have a penchant for numbers, but I remember to this day what we paid for the house.

Two years after we moved in, we had a third child, James. Our boys shared a room for a couple of years, but we soon added on another bedroom and a family room for our growing family. James got excited when the "pounding men came" and took the windows away and knocked down the walls. We loved the new addition, especially the family room where our kids could spread out their toys and play. Bit by bit we changed the house and made it ours: new carpet on the stairs, calmer colors on the walls, and tiny pink hearts to replace the plaid in our daughter's room.

Five years after the first big addition, we took a deep breath and remodeled the kitchen. The pounding men returned and took the walls down to the studs. We somehow managed to feed the family using a toaster oven and microwave during the dusty days of demolition. Some nights we gave up and ordered pizza. No one minded using paper plates, since that meant no one had to wash the dishes.

Gradually, the house took shape. We stopped talking about making more big changes. The house suited us and our family of five. Three kids with varying interests and obligations: basketball practice, friends, tap lessons, rehearsals, birthday parties.

☙

IN OCTOBER OF 1991 CAITLIN WAS THIRTEEN, ALMOST fourteen, and in middle school; Myles was ten, almost eleven, in fifth grade; and James was five and a half, in his first year of school.

First day of school, September, 1991

Both of my older kids have December birthdays, which makes for a lot of excitement at the end of the year. We threw a lot of birthday parties, with silly games and special cakes, and celebrated Hanukkah (with my family) and Christmas (with Bruce's). Caitlin had entered the world of middle school and teenage angst. We didn't have as many battles as my mother and I did, but this was the beginning of her quest for more independence, her interest in boys, and her desire to define herself outside of the family. She joined the basketball team at school, which added a new layer of logistics to our family routine. Myles had tap class after school, so there were trips to

Berkeley once a week. James, as the youngest with no plans of his own, had to tag along on these jaunts.

The year Caitlin turned fourteen began the annual exchange of the velvet painting of Elvis. Bruce and I purchased a late-in-his-career likeness of the King in Tijuana, on a side trip from San Diego. Since Caitlin was born the year Elvis died, we'd decided that she would appreciate the piece of art we'd haggled for with a street vendor. On the morning of her birthday, we left a huge box (labeled nineteen-inch television) on the counter with a birthday card addressed to her. She tore open the box, tossed aside the crumpled newspapers packed in layers, and pulled out the velvet painting. She laughed long and hard and then plotted her revenge. The following June, Bruce received the painting, wrapped in the funnies, for his birthday. He brought it to his San Francisco office, which is how the painting survived the fire that year. And so the tradition continues. To this day, Elvis spends half the year with Bruce and half the year with Caitlin.

Because we lived across the street from the school, Bruce and I got involved in fundraising activities and helped organize the walk-a-thon. In a moment of weakness, I got elected PTA president. We became part of a group of parents who enjoyed each other's company at parties or picnics. We played softball and flew kites with our kids. The school community had become our community.

We had finally reached a point where we felt settled and engaged in our neighborhood. We'd figured out how to have fun, do good work, raise our family in a home we loved, and looked forward to many happy years in our big blue house.

CHAPTER TWO

SUNDAY

Morning, October 20

That Sunday had started out unremarkably: pancakes for breakfast, a little extra coffee, newspapers scattered across the table, Caitlin working on a poster project for school in the living room, James watching *The Little Mermaid* in the family room, Myles playing at a friend's house nearby.

As we lingered over a second cup of coffee, Bruce and I looked out the window and noticed ashes swirling in the backyard, little dervishes of black flakes. The window was open, and we smelled smoke. Sunday morning: too early for barbecue. And this was a different kind of smoke anyway. It smelled like an old ashtray: whiffs of sulfur, sharp enough to hurt your nose and throat. Was someone's house on fire? Maybe a tree was burning? Bruce turned on the radio to see if there was news about a fire. We'd heard the news the day before, on Saturday—about a fire that had started in the hills above the Caldecott Tunnel, a mile and a half away. James and I had seen the helicopters flying overhead with buckets of water suspended from their bellies. The firefighters had put it out, though—hadn't they?

But the radio announcer was saying that firefighters had discovered hot embers, left smoldering for hours. Then the wind had kicked up. The hills were on fire.

Bruce and I walked outside and scanned the sky for smoke. It was coming from higher up the hill and blowing west, toward us. We couldn't see what was burning from the sidewalk in front of our house, so we headed up the hill to get a better look. Our neighborhood was a collection of mismatched houses in styles that varied from Tudor-style cottages to big-shouldered boxes, many of which were barely visible behind tall trees and shrubs. One of the houses on our block used to be a hunting lodge, according to a longtime resident. The bowl-like shape of the school's playground used to be a pond. Underground creeks still ran downhill, creating drainage problems for the houses on our flat block.

We lived at the beginning of the increasingly steep incline of Broadway Terrace, a street that led up to the hills over the Caldecott Tunnel. I used to walk partway up that hill, with the kids, for picnics or playtime at Lake Temescal, with its sandy beach and big lawns.

In the early 1900s the Oakland hills were oak savannah/grassland, with native bunch grasses and nonnative annual grasses, coyote brush, manzanita and other coastal scrub plants. Probably there were bay trees and buckeyes in the wet areas. Then, the eucalyptus and Monterey pine planted early in the century spread everywhere, and those—plus the horrid blackwood acacia—took over. At the time of the fire, those trees were dominating the hills, but were mixed with a lot of aging exotics planted by homeowners, plus coyote brush and Scotch and French broom. All of it tinder.

As Bruce and I walked up the hill on Broadway Terrace that morning, we saw how the black smoke rose high over the tunnel; the hills surrounding it were ablaze. Hiller Highlands, a community of condominiums that hugged the hillside above us—across eight lanes of highway—was burning. The joined buildings stood in clusters at the crest of the hills, and they were burning faster than our minds could comprehend. The fire looked like it could devour the entire hillside in a matter of minutes. But it couldn't jump the freeway, we assured each other. Could it?

Bruce and I stopped walking before we got to the entrance to the lake. Most of the neighbors would be home on a Sunday morning, but we heard later about some who had gone sailing on the bay, or hiking in Marin, or to a family birthday party in Walnut Creek. They said they could see bits of ash and a column of black smoke from miles away.

People came out of their houses and stood on the sidewalk, facing east, shielding their eyes against the fluttering ash, stinging smoke, and bright sun. The wind seemed to pick up speed as we stood there, and now we could hear the fire as it snapped at rooftops and trees. Everyone we saw along the way —some we knew from school or had seen at the neighborhood market—had some news to share: it was the fire from yesterday that didn't really get extinguished; we would be safe on our side of the freeway; no chance it would jump the freeway and spread down the hill; of course it would jump the freeway—don't you feel that wind? We didn't know whom to believe. We exchanged concerned glances with our neighbors as we passed them, standing and watching, some with hoses at the ready, just in case.

Questions floated through the air like the ashes. How could this be happening? Look how many houses are on fire. But it was still so far away from us, wasn't it? Should we leave our houses or should we stay? Then, like the others, we stood and watched for several moments, trying to decide. Some guy with a radio held up his hand and gave us an update. "They say with this wind blowing, there's no telling what's going to stop it. That fire could jump the freeway easy."

The heat, the wind, the burning embers buzzing past us like fireflies, the sight of so many homes already engulfed in angry flames—it was happening so fast. I reached for my husband's hand.

When we walked up the hill just moments before, we were curious spectators. On the way down the hill, on our way back home to where we'd left Caitlin and James huddled together in front of a movie—without even saying a word—we both knew we would have to evacuate.

"I'll start throwing stuff in the car," I said.

"I'll call my folks," he replied. "We can wait it out over there."

We didn't want to wait and see what happened if the fire got any closer. With smoke making our eyes water and bits of ash now clinging to our clothes, we knew we had to leave as soon as we could. Neither of us really believed the fire would reach our house. I remember the feeling of watching and not comprehending—yes, the hills were on fire, it was only a mile away, but still, this couldn't be happening, could it? A full-blown firestorm this close to my house, my block, the school, our little world of routines: homework, dinner, Halloween costumes, tap lessons, kindergarten, middle school dances, and birthday parties? What would happen to all that? But we couldn't do anything except pack up a few things and leave. Bruce believed we'd stay overnight with his folks and come back the next day, back to our unscathed house. I wanted to make sure I didn't leave anything I couldn't replace behind. I wish now that I'd thought more about what I chose to take with me.

We hurried back home, talking along the way about what we'd take with us. We'd bring the photo albums lined up in rows on bookshelves in the family room and the baby books I'd put together for each of the three kids. I'd make sure James took his special blanket and favorite stuffed toys, pj's, and his toothbrush. I'd have to call Myles's friend's parents and let them know I'd be over to pick him up early. Although he'd been looking forward to spending the day with his friend and her family—he always had fun over there—that plan would have to change. Of course, he had to come with us and be together with his family. Bruce would back up the computer and see if he could wet down the roof, as some of the neighbors were already doing. I would take the kids in my car. He would stay behind, grab a few more things, and follow behind us in his car. We were thinking faster than we could talk, overlapping what we were saying and finishing each other's sentences. We covered everything we could think of, and once we got in the house again, we would pick up speed and begin our evacuation.

When we got back to our block, I saw my good friend Chris and her husband, John, half a block away in front of their house. They were standing out on the sidewalk, shading their eyes with their hands, looking toward the hills.

"Are you leaving?" Chris asked.

"It looks like it's going to jump the freeway," I said. "A guy heard it on the radio. I don't know . . . it's looking pretty bad up there." And then I said, "We're packing up the cars." They shook their heads, and Chris said, "Really?"

"You can't believe what's happening up there," I said. "I don't want the kids to get scared, and I don't want to wait to be told to evacuate. So we're throwing stuff in the cars and getting away. Are you guys leaving?"

"If you are," Chris said, and looked at John. They started back up the steps to their house.

Other neighbors came outside: the older woman from next door, who had just lost her husband in August. They'd been on the block for more than thirty-five years, and now she lived alone. And the nice couple from three houses up, dapper silver-haired Mario—who washed his car in the driveway every weekend—stood looking up the hill to where the fire raged.

We rushed inside. My daughter had the radio on, and the news frightened her. "Mom, what are we going to do? Are we going to leave?" Both kids were very quiet. The bits of ash continued to float onto our patio, clearly visible through the windows. They looked to me for answers.

"I'll take you guys and Ethel's birdcage, and we'll go pick up Myles at Kelly's house. We're going to be together, and we'll go someplace safe." Bruce called his parents, who lived twenty minutes away, and asked if we could come over. Surprised, they said yes; they hadn't heard yet about the fire.

We told the kids we were all going to stay with Nana and Poppa until it was safe to come home, and sent them upstairs to collect a few things to take with them. Caitlin put her Birkenstocks and her schoolbooks in her backpack. She'd paid for the sandals with her own money, and she wasn't leaving them behind. I went into Myles's room and grabbed his tap shoes but nothing else. Bruce and I ran through the rest of the house, thinking fast. I took armfuls of photo albums and put them into the back of my car. It took several trips to get them all. Then I got the baby books, and our bird, Ethel, and brought them down to the car. I thought for a moment about our cat, who'd died a couple of months before, and felt grateful, since she was feeble and wouldn't have managed such a sudden transition to my in-laws' house, especially since they had a dog. No one thought to bring a change of clothes. Or the pictures on the mantel or the ones on the wall, the ones we loved to look at every day.

I looked around my bedroom. My jewelry box—full of the everyday earrings I wore—I left behind. I took the "good" jewelry box, a gift from Bruce years before, full of pieces I rarely looked at or had occasion to wear. The gold bangle bracelet I wore at my wedding was in that box. It was the only thing I had from the grandmother who died before I was born. The pearls I got when I was thirteen were in there, along with a yellowed square of newspaper that contained my grand-father's obituary. Another faded scrap of paper: a letter to the editor I'd written about the first baseball game I'd ever attended. Some ribbons from my dad's Army uniform were in there too. I tucked the box under my arm and left the bedroom, stopping to look in James's and Caitlin's rooms as I rushed to get everything in the car. Caitlin looked at her aquarium, and said goodbye to her fish. I told James we would bring his blanket and his favorite fuzzy snowman so he would have them in case we needed to stay overnight at Nana and Poppa's.

We flipped back and forth between being in denial and acknowledging the power of wind and fire. If we were packing up just for a fire drill, we wouldn't bring things like clothes and shoes, important papers, and family mementos. And we didn't bring those things, choosing—even in the face of facts we couldn't yet comprehend—to believe we'd be back later, or possibly the next day, and would feel silly about running away like this when the fire wouldn't reach us, couldn't reach us. It was still far away.

But I grabbed my leather jacket out of the hall closet, even though it was hot, so hot, outside. I loved that jacket. It had been a birthday present from Bruce the year before, and I didn't want to leave it behind, in case. . . .

I did not think to bring certain things: my wedding dress and pressed flowers from the bouquet I carried; the pictures of my daughter's birth that were, we thought, in a safe place—tucked away in a metal box in a cupboard in the garage. Some long-lost baby pictures of my husband. And the box of old pictures he'd found stuffed in the back of an office drawer, taken after the 1906 earthquake and fire. These photographs showed people in the streets of San Francisco, cooking over open fires on makeshift stoves. You could see the remains of the city in the background. Messages written in chalk on pieces of wood, offering rides to Oakland. We'd always intended to donate these photographs to a museum someday. Instead, they were forgotten in a box in the garage. Hadn't looked at them in years but never forgot the spirit in those images of hardy survivors, living by their wits after a disaster had destroyed their homes and their lives.

WE'D AGREED THAT I WOULD GET MYLES AND LEAVE THE area in my car, and Bruce would follow shortly afterward, even though we hadn't been told yet to evacuate. I called Myles's friend's parents and let them know I was on my way. The friend's father said something on the phone about taking the kids to the park, but I said no, I needed to bring him with us, away from the fire. I had to have all my children with me, I said. They lived just a few blocks away, so I arrived soon after my call.

I got out of the car and gave Myles a hug. He looked like he was fighting tears, and I could hear the fear in his voice.

"Will our house burn?" he asked. By then, the black smoke filled the sky to the east and billowed over the hills.

"I don't know," I said, "I hope it doesn't. Nobody knows how long it'll take to put the fire out, so we're going over to Nana and Poppa's house tonight, just to be on the safe side." Then I added, "I grabbed your tap shoes. We're not bringing all our stuff, but I thought you'd want your shoes." He tried to give me a smile, but I realized even in that moment how little comfort his shoes would bring him if we were to lose everything.

He got in the backseat, next to his brother, and we drove away.

Bruce promised he wouldn't stay behind long. No heroics, we agreed. He remembers spraying the roof and watching the water evaporate immediately. After coiling up the hose at the side of the house, he came inside, grabbed the binder with our collection of favorite recipes, sat down at the computer and downloaded some things onto a small disc, then got in his car and drove to meet us, leaving the house to its fate.

_____

CHAPTER THREE

NOT KNOWING

Sunday, 1:00 p.m.

I drove a few miles north to El Cerrito, to my in-laws' house, expecting to spend the night and go home the next day. That evening, my father-in-law prepared one of his famous casseroles for dinner, and my mother-in-law helped get us settled in—all five of us, plus the bird. Bruce and I made up the sofa bed in the book-lined study. The boys would bunk in the twin beds in the guest room. Caitlin would make do on the sofa in the living room. My in-laws' dog made Ethel nervous, so we kept her cage in our room with the door closed.

We had left in such a hurry that we hadn't packed our toothbrushes, toothpaste, or other essentials, so Bruce and I headed out to the local Longs drugstore to buy supplies, including T-shirts and changes of socks and underwear. James was the only one to have packed a toothbrush, so we just needed four. We roamed each aisle, tossing things into the cart. How many pairs of socks? Should we buy more T-shirts? Shampoo? Not knowing if we needed one change of clothes or five, or more, we bought just enough to get us through the next couple of days.

It had been a hot day, and Bruce left the house wearing a pair of shorts, but the night had turned cold. Given the choice, and the right climate, he would always wear shorts. ("Could've worn shorts" is something you could always count on him to say whenever he spent time outdoors in long pants. Part of his optimism about returning home sooner rather than later was reflected in his choice to leave his jeans behind.) We found a pair of sweatpants and a sweatshirt, and he threw them in the cart, too. He hated to admit he was cold, but he was cold. We split up down the aisles and tossed Fruit of the Looms, packages of tube socks, and deodorant into our carts.

BACK AT MY IN-LAWS' HOUSE, WE LOOKED OUT THE large picture window that faced directly south toward Oakland. From high in the El Cerrito hills, we could see the outline of the fire, jagged orange lines silhouetting the hillsides behind the Campanile on the Berkeley campus, above the white towers of the Claremont Hotel. We walked back and forth between the television in the family room and the picture window in the living room every ten minutes, trying to reconcile what we were looking at with what we could recognize. Was our house burning? Had it burned down already? What had we left behind that we should have taken? What about our friends and neighbors?

The uncertainty mounted as the hours went by. We saw the same footage from earlier in the day over and over, and shuddered as we saw the damage already done by the raging fire.

My in-laws left us alone for the most part. My normally upbeat and positive mother-in-law, Marilyn, seemed at a loss for words. Her New England stoicism had helped me so much when I was at my lowest point during Caitlin's hospitalization. One day, I had called her and couldn't even speak before I burst into tears. She calmly told me to "just hang on." Her voice, steady and strong that day, helped me collect myself and carry on through another difficult stretch of hours at my baby's bedside.

John, my father-in-law, was quiet, preferring to putter around the kitchen and offer us food and drinks. That's where he felt most comfortable, at the stove or the cutting board on the counter, leaving the conversation to others. I was so intent on trying to figure out what I was looking at out the window and on TV that I couldn't make any effort toward polite conversation with either of them.

The kids had scattered, grabbing books off the shelves and retreating to quiet parts of the house.

Watching the news that night, we couldn't tell if we had a home to go back to or not. We tried to get a fix on where the reporters were standing during their updates. Shouting into their microphones over the wind, they stood beneath street signs we couldn't quite make out the names of. Getting closer to the television didn't help. At one point we were certain we saw our neighbors' elegant white house in flames, thought we saw their entire block burning, and felt so bad for them. "That looks like Broadway Terrace, doesn't it?" I said. We stared at the screen but couldn't be certain what we saw. If it was their house, we wondered whether they had much time to evacuate, or if they were even home. If their house was gone, maybe the fire hadn't jumped across the wide expanse between their house and ours. Maybe our block would be spared after all. We were a tiny bit hopeful. Was this denial? Denial had gotten us through some tough times before and maybe it would again. There was so much we didn't know.

THE KIDS' NORMAL BEDTIME ROUTINE GOT OVERLOOKED that night. No one read a story to James, and I don't think we even tucked the kids in. We always read stories at bedtime, always tucked the kids in, or at least made sure to say, "Goodnight, sleep tight." But that night, the boys put themselves to bed in the guest room. James buried his face in his blanket and held onto his snowman toy, but Myles was missing his cat blanket, one of the many important belongings that ended up getting left behind.

He came into the family room, where we were watching news of the fire, and asked, "Did you guys bring my cat blanket?"

I hadn't thought to bring it and neither had Bruce. Except for sleepaway camp in the summer, this was the first time in his life he'd gone to bed without the handmade quilt that featured a family of cats curled up together beneath a starry sky. How could I have grabbed his tap shoes but not that blanket?

"No, buddy," I said. "I'm so sorry." He turned around and went back to bed. And at that moment I knew how much he needed that one reminder of home. There wasn't anything I could do to make it better. Sure, he was a big kid, but that blanket had been a baby gift from a friend, and we all knew how much he loved it. We had pictures of him and James and that blanket, taken all over the house. He may not have wanted to admit how much it meant to him, thinking it might seem babyish, but—and I knew this all along—he was a kid who had always showed a resistance to change. Now, suddenly, it was possible that everything had changed, and he was without his lifelong source of comfort. I knew I could live without many of my things if I had to, but I felt as though I had unthinkingly left behind something terribly important to my son.

Caitlin settled in on the couch in the living room. From her vantage point on her makeshift bed, she was able to look out the window and see the line of the fire against the black hills long into the night. I hated to leave her in there by herself as we spread out for the night. It must have been terrifying for her to face that sight alone, but there was nowhere else for her to sleep, and she was probably just as exhausted as we were. "Will you be okay out here?" I asked her. "You don't have any privacy."

She said she'd be fine. No one got a proper goodnight. I just hoped they were able to fall asleep. I doubted I would be able to.

I couldn't stop my thoughts from racing through the events of the day, and I couldn't get the last moments we spent in the house out of my mind.

The image of Caitlin earlier that day stuck with me. As we'd driven away from our house, she'd looked to the flaming, smoky hills and then back to me behind the wheel. Her two brothers and the bird were still sitting quietly in the backseat. No one spoke. And then she'd said, "Mom, you're being so strong." I wondered what she saw to make her think so.

ONCE THE KIDS WERE SETTLED IN THEIR MAKESHIFT bedrooms, I borrowed a nightgown and robe from my mother-in-law. It was an awkward moment, never having borrowed so much as a sweater from her before. She made the offer, and I accepted gratefully. I hadn't thought to bring anything to wear to bed that night. On the thin mattress of the sofa bed Bruce and I stared at the ceiling for a long time, side by side. I couldn't sleep. What if? What if? What if?

I got up in the darkness, checked the clock in the kitchen. It was 4 a.m. I crept around the house in my borrowed robe, gathering the things the kids had worn the day before, and started some laundry. John, always an early riser, was already awake. He'd made a pot of coffee and silently offered me a cup. "What'll you have for breakfast?" he asked, and started pulling out eggs, bread, cereal, and milk.

CHAPTER FOUR

FINDING OUT

October 22

By now, two days later, we had begun to comprehend the vast toll of the fire—in human lives, acres scorched, homes lost: fourteen confirmed deaths, at least twenty-five people still missing, 1,800 acres destroyed, 5,000 people evacuated, 2,000 houses and apartments burned. All of these numbers would climb in the coming days.

We left the kids with their grandparents and drove back to Oakland. The elementary school was closed, and no one at his office expected Bruce to show up. We had to find out, finally, what had happened to our house. Bruce had a phone in his car —we didn't have cell phones then—and we used the moments of privacy on the ride over to the neighborhood to check in with friends and family and let them know where we were staying.

My sister lived just a few minutes away from us, up Broadway Terrace, high in the hills. She'd been visiting with friends on Sunday. I'd grabbed a few cards from my Rolodex on my way out of the house, and because she'd told me which friend she was going to be with that day, I had her phone number with me. I'd contacted my sister once we got to safety on Sunday, but neither of us knew if we had homes to go back to. She ended up staying at her friend's house for several days.

I called her again from the car. "Do you know if your house is okay?" I asked her. She'd learned that one of her neighbors had fought off sparks and flying embers with a hose and a bucket brigade with other neighbors. Her block had survived intact. Good news. I was especially concerned because her house was surrounded by eucalyptus and might have been impossible for firefighters to reach if the fire had spread to the canyon below her. Her street was narrow, high up in the hills, and the house clung to the hillside on stilts. I said that I hoped our news would be good too, but I had no information yet.

I told her we were on our way back to the neighborhood. She started to say something and stopped herself. Then she said, "It doesn't look good."

"What do you mean?" I asked. My heartbeat quickened.

"Just . . . it doesn't look good."

She knew—and she couldn't tell me. I understood suddenly what must have happened. Someone had seen our house and told her something, but she didn't want to be the one to share bad news.

And then my stomach flipped. "We're almost there. I have to get off the phone," I said. I hung up and looked over at Bruce.

"She says it doesn't look good. She couldn't tell me that she already knew."

〜

WE JOINED THE GROUP OF NEIGHBORS GATHERED AT THE foot of Broadway Terrace, peering over yellow police tape, hoping for news. I saw our neighbor Mario's wife, Florence, over near the corner where a policeman was holding the line of people back, his palms raised.

Florence saw me and came over to where we were standing. She gave me a big hug. "Oh, honey," she said, "it's all gone."

No one was allowed to cross the yellow tape and go up the hill to our houses. So a small group of us milled around for a while, asking about the other neighbors and sharing what we'd heard. The crowd on the corner thinned out after about half an hour. We got back in the car and headed to my in-laws' house.

Over the next few days, we heard more stories about the day of the fire. We learned that our widowed next-door neighbor had been visiting her children, celebrating what would have been her husband's seventy-fifth birthday. She wasn't home the afternoon of the fire and didn't have a chance to get anything from her house. All her photos, everything— she lost it all, including the cash her husband had insisted keeping in the house in case of an emergency.

Chris, my neighbor from up the street, told me that she and her family had gone to stay with friends. They evacuated much later than we did. She also told me that her husband had packed all of her shoes, some of her work clothes, and her strapless bra. "I never even wear that strapless bra," she told me. "What could he have been thinking?" What were any of us thinking when we ran out?

A friend told me that she'd stopped loading furniture and clothes into her car as she watched our block burn. "I saw all the houses go," she told me. "I saw Chris's piano fall through the floor, down to the basement. The roof caught and then, boom, it was just gone," she said.

Some of our friends and family had reached us in El Cerrito to find out how we were. We had already amassed a stack of pink "while you were out" messages from people who guessed where we were staying. Other concerned friends told us they'd called our house but didn't get an answer. They figured if the phone rang, the house was still there. Well, it rang somewhere, I guess, but according to the maps we saw later, by about 4:00 p.m. on that Sunday, we no longer had a home.

ON THE WAY BACK TO MY IN-LAWS', WE REHEARSED WHAT we would tell the kids. We couldn't protect them from the truth, now that we knew it. What would it mean to James? Would he understand that we wouldn't be able to go home, that he couldn't hold hands with Myles and cross the street to school anymore? For how long? And how would the big kids react? Caitlin and Myles would have a tougher time with the uncertainty and the changes. We couldn't sugarcoat the news: our house was gone, our neighborhood was gone, and we didn't have a plan. Except for this: we decided to rebuild our house right where it was.

"I don't want to live anywhere else, do you?" Bruce asked.

"No," I said.

WHEN WE ARRIVED BACK AT MY IN-LAWS' HOUSE, IT WAS time for a family conversation, just the five of us. Bruce said, "Listen you guys. We found out that our house—our whole block probably—burned in the fire. We can't go back there to see it until the police say it's okay."

I said, "We're going to figure out a place we can stay on our own as soon as we can." The kids wanted to know where we would live and where they would sleep and whether we could go back and get any of our stuff.

We promised them that we would build another house, and we would have a place of our own to live in soon. James was matter-of-fact about it, but the older kids had a million questions. What about school? Who was going to help us? We didn't have answers for them then. We wanted to know the same things. I felt as though the feelings of uncertainty rose from my gut to my throat, but the words that came out were calm and reassuring. I had to tamp down the stress I was feeling so the kids wouldn't see how out of control the situation was right then.

Caitlin told me she'd imagined the fire going through the house like a burglar, touching everything and deciding to take it all. She worried about the fish in her fish tank, left behind to their fiery fate. She understood that we couldn't save them. And when she said that, about a burglar going through all her things and how she felt violated, I thought about it too. But the image is all wrong. A burglar might take his time, looking at everything and deciding what to take, maybe missing some things that had been hidden well or locked away.

We learned that it takes less than half a minute for an entire house to burn to the ground: just eleven seconds for a roof to catch, the windows to blow out, and the structure to totally collapse. It was more like a bomb dropping on the house: everything gone all at once. By the time you hear the whistle of the falling bomb, it's all over. As for the fish, I imagine the glass exploded from the heat, the water gushed out, and then there was nothing but ash. We heard later on about how people spent days searching for their pets that were left to fend for themselves that day. There wasn't much point in worrying about the fish.

CHAPTER FIVE

CHIMNEYS

October 23

Back at the foot of Broadway Terrace, I squeezed into a police car with another couple. No homeowners were allowed to drive themselves in yet; hazardous sparks and hot spots still glowed in some places. Fallen power lines might still be live. Each car had room for three people, so the pairings were random. We had the conversation I would have with people for the next days, weeks, months and years: Where was your house? Were you home? What did you take? But as the car approached the neighborhoods that had been leveled by the fire, we stopped talking and gawked out the windows. We rode in silence, afraid and anxious to get close enough to see what remained of our homes and our streets. I felt very much alone, even with the officer and this other couple sitting in the car with me.

Bruce had elected to spend the day on the phone with our insurance company and the bank, and attend to the business of getting our records. One of the decisions we made early on was to divide up certain tasks between us. He felt comfortable dealing with the insurance and the other institutions that needed to be contacted. I would eventually take on much bigger jobs, but I was willing to make the first inspection of the remains of the house. It wasn't until recently that he told me the real reason he didn't come with me: he was afraid to see what was left. I was scared too. Some reports said that everything that could have burned, did. Still, I didn't know quite what to expect.

It was so odd. Things at the bottom of the hill had looked normal. Houses, cars, the golf course, blocks of undisturbed homes left untouched by the fire. But then, a block or so farther up, the devastation came into view.

The first thing I noticed were the chimneys, tall brick columns still attached to their hearths, punctuating wide expanses of black, all the way up to the top of the hills. And it was quiet. No birds, no other cars, no people.

The hills of our destroyed neighborhood resembled a moonscape: a postapocalyptic expanse of scorched earth, blackened trees, and chimneys standing like sentinels left to watch over the ruins. Gray foundations marked the footprints of houses no longer there. We were shocked at the vastness of the damage. Stone cherubs stood in what had been a backyard; a fountain survived surrounded by ashes; skeletons were all that remained of the patio furniture.

As the police car rounded the corner onto our street, I felt a hard knot forming in my stomach.

I looked out the window for a familiar landmark: our

neighbor's fence, the house high up the hill that used to be a hunting lodge years ago. But there weren't any landmarks. I wasn't sure anymore if it was my street.

The car crept along slowly, and the woman sitting next to me in the backseat reached out and squeezed my hand. The car came to a stop across from the school. On my right, the school still stood, the fence was there, the playground was intact. I looked to my left, then, toward the house.

Oh, but that couldn't be right. No.

I got out of the car and took a closer look.

Our house had fallen in on itself. Standing in the driveway, I could see uphill into the backyard, right past where the walls had once stood, right past where the kitchen had been, where the kids ate their cereal in the morning, right past what used to be the living room where we put up our Christmas tree each year. Only metal remained recognizable: bedsprings, shells of the appliances, frames of our outdoor chairs. Everything else was splintered, blackened, reduced to ash and unrecognizable bits. The barbeque was there, in the back, where the wooden deck had been. But the rest—the house, the trees, the fence—it was all gone.

And then I noticed the red brick planters, the ones that held the daffodils each spring, and there was our mailbox, untouched by the fire.

My legs started shaking, I felt a little dizzy—like I might be sick to my stomach. My brain couldn't process what my eyes were seeing. I hated standing there in front of strangers, witnessing the wreckage, finally understanding that there would be nothing left to save. I wished Bruce had come with me.

HE WENT BACK A FEW DAYS LATER TO SEE FOR HIMSELF.
I'd prepared him as much as I could. It took him a while to
steel himself for the sight. His normally optimistic outlook had
kept him in denial longer than I would have expected, but he
finally had to go back and face reality.

He'd bought some coveralls to wear as he walked around looking for anything that might have survived the extreme temperature. Inside the blackened shell of our dishwasher he found some coffee mugs from our interrupted Sunday morning —my daughter remembers that one of the mugs had a scene from our favorite movie, *Gone with the Wind*, on it. We saw that movie together when she was around twelve, and one of us gave the mug to the other for Christmas that year.

Bruce also found an oddly shaped sculpture, formed from melted glass folded over itself in layers, like a ruffled skirt, with openings at both ends. The glass holds impressions of the tines of a fork; a tiny chunk of charcoal hides within its hardened folds. A spoon juts out of one of the curved ends.

This delicate, fire-hardened sculpture remains the only artifact we have from the house. We kept the mugs, but abandoned them after a week or two. No one wanted to use them.

CHAPTER SIX

LISTS

Our insurance agent told us we needed to compile a list of everything we'd had in the house in order to be reimbursed for replacement costs. We were lucky to have made the decision to purchase this type of insurance the previous year when we renewed our policy. It had been inexpensive to add, and we'd hardly given it a second thought. Now, if we could just provide the actual purchase price of these items and then somehow calculate the replacement cost, the insurance company would cut us a check. So the lifetime accumulations of two forty-year-old adults, plus the possessions of three children, ages fourteen, eleven, and five, had to be quantified and put on a spreadsheet. Everything—from socks and underwear to plates, cups, knives, tools, hats and coats, artwork, and odds and ends—from attic to garage in a four-bedroom house had to be broken down.

The list ran to around forty-six pages, single-spaced.

How much stuff could a five-year-old have? Here's an excerpt from the two and a half pages for James:

A "Good for Me!" chart

4 shelves of children's
  books

40 audio story tapes

Activity books

Baseball hat

Boots

Bubble Blaster

Chalkboard

Crayons

Easel and paints

Fisher-Price binoculars

Growth chart

Gumball-machine lamp

Hand-quilted wall
  hanging

Happy Today pillow

Hat rack

Legos

Little cars and trucks

Little table with two
  benches

Night-light

Pajamas

Passport

Plastic tool set

Puppet theater

Rain slicker

Shirts

Shoes

Shorts

Socks

Stamp-a-Story set

Stuffed animals

Sweatshirts

Tool bench

Toy guitar

Wooden puzzles

We made lists like this for all of us. We had to mentally walk through the house, maybe consulting the photo albums for reminders, but mostly working from memory. The posters and prints we'd hung on the walls and looked at every day: everything from Picasso to the whimsical watercolor paintings of our cats. Things we'd touched or seen every day, some of them for a lifetime, long forgotten until I recently found this list, packed away along with newspapers from the days and weeks after the fire.

This excerpt from Caitlin's list speaks to her young-teen status:

Baseball caps	Lipsticks
Charm bracelet	Music box
Clock radio	Posters
Cosmetics	Telephone
Dolls and stuffed	Tennis racquet
animals	Thesaurus
Dresses	Wooden chess set
Earrings	Wreath with flowers
Felt fedora	Yo-yo
Fish and two-gallon	
fish tank	

THE SUMMER BEFORE THE FIRE, BRUCE BOUGHT ME A book on how to get rid of clutter around the house. I'd read the book and had launched a cleanup campaign that involved every room in the house. I'd inventoried every pot and pan, every cookie sheet, every remnant of fabric and ball of yarn. The kids had to get rid of old toys and games, and I gave away a lot of too-small clothes and kitchen duplicates. So, in a sense, I had prepared myself to make the list the insurance agent wanted.

I knew how many shoe boxes I had in my closet. I knew we had six cookie sheets and seven beach towels and two white tablecloths. It's all there, on the list. Forty-six pages long. What we had. What we lost.

Everything.

PART 2

CHAPTER   SEVEN

MOVING

A good friend who had left Oakland and moved to Moraga (a suburb on the other side of the hills) tracked me down at my in-laws' and gave me the phone number of a realtor friend of hers. "Call him right away," she said. "You need to get out there now and start looking. You'll never find a big enough house to rent in Oakland."

We ended up staying with my in-laws for a week after the fire while we looked at rental houses and tried to figure out where to move.

In Moraga, we looked at five or six houses, rushing from one to the next from the list we got from the realtor. We looked at large houses with big yards and one that even had a pool. At each house we saw other families from our neighborhood, all with the same haunted looks on their faces, the same thrown-together outfits, the dark circles under their eyes, the same story as ours. We were zombies, looking for a place to sleep and settle in with our families. We didn't have the luxury of taking our time to weigh the options. A local realtor reported getting calls from eighty to ninety Oakland families a day, all looking for houses to rent. Other people would snap up the best places if we didn't act quickly.

When we got back to my in-laws' at the end of a busy day of looking at houses and making decisions that would have an effect on our immediate future, we tried to return all the phone messages that had stacked up. We had to answer the same questions over and over: What did you take? When did you know? Did you have insurance? Was anything left? How are the kids doing?

It was exhausting.

We felt grateful that Bruce's parents took us in, but their hospitality came with a price.

One night I arrived late for dinner. I'd been doing errands and had stopped to see a friend for a hug and a cry. My father-in-law, who always cooked for the family, didn't like dinner to be late. Even though I'd called and told Bruce to let everyone know they could start without me, his father insisted on waiting. He was like that—rigid about certain things. When Bruce was growing up, his father cooked eggs on Wednesdays and Saturdays, pancakes or waffles on Sundays. Now there was cocktail hour before dinner and an old ship's bell from his Navy days to call everyone in to dinner. He didn't like his routine to be disrupted, even under unusual circumstances, like having a house full of displaced family members.

"Just tell him to go ahead," I'd said to Bruce, calling from my friend's house. "I don't want to come back yet. I need to see my friends."

"Please. Get here as soon as you can," he replied. I could hear the stress in his voice. His father was a kind man, but I knew how he could get when he was irritated: the tone of voice, the tight lips, the muttering under his breath. It was easy to tell when he wasn't pleased.

When I got to their house, already wrung out, only to discover that I was in trouble for being late for dinner, I felt betrayed. Bruce was supposed to smooth it over for me, and instead, I had to slink in and apologize for making everyone else wait. I had grown accustomed in a very short time to the understanding and kindness we'd been shown by everyone— from shopkeepers and salesclerks to strangers. To be scolded and made to feel as though I'd been intentionally thoughtless felt like a slap to the face. Behind closed doors that night, Bruce and I went over it again.

"How come he pitched a fit about dinner?" I asked. "I need to do what's right for me. Why is he making this harder?" We needed nurturing and support, not curfews and guilt-trips.

We both ended up in tears. How could we act like adults when we were being treated like children? We needed to get back to being our own little family—and soon.

WE HAD MAJOR DECISIONS TO MAKE: WHERE TO LIVE, how to deal with insurance, how to rebuild the house, how to share the endless tasks ahead. We needed privacy and time, both of which were in short supply with everyone underfoot. And though we felt welcome, we also felt the awkwardness of imposing on my in-laws. They suddenly had a more-than-full house of people, plus one bird. The pile of pink message slips meant that the phone rang incessantly and the calls were for us, not them. They were thrust into the role of caretakers and secretaries, and though they seemed to do it willingly, we couldn't avoid feeling the tension.

The day following the dinner incident, Bruce and I drove back toward Oakland through Berkeley, still upset from the night before. The traffic slowed as we approached the fire zone. Other drivers craned their necks to get a better look at the blackened hillsides and moved along at a maddeningly slow crawl.

"Damned looky-loos!" Bruce yelled. And then he pounded the steering wheel and cried, "Things will never be the same!" He'd held himself together until that moment, moving forward and taking control of what he could. But all at once, the scope of our loss and the helplessness we both felt inside burst out of him. He started to sob, but still managed to keep driving—shaking and wailing—until I begged him to stop the car. He pulled over, and I just held him.

CHAPTER EIGHT

THE NEWS

All the local papers were full of news about the fire. There were stories about heroes and stories about tragic twists of fate and stories about lost pets. I saved a week's worth of newspapers. Reading them again now brings back the horror of those first few days, when no one knew how many died, or how many houses were lost, or what the damages were. The stories kept coming about bravery, sacrifice, and unfathomable destruction.

I've since read official reports describing how firefighters were helpless in their attempts to suppress the fire; how residents got trapped, encircled by flames, blinded by smoke, as they tried desperately to escape the fire. Firefighters fought for their lives. In televised footage taken of the neighborhood going up in flames you can hear one of them saying, "I've never seen anything like this."

A technical report published by the US Fire Administration describes "flaming whirlwinds" and "rolling clouds of fire moving through the air or along the ground." When bodies were found, it was clear that people died in the streets trying to outrun the flames. A police officer was identified by the serial number on his gear, the fire battalion chief by his helmet. One report said most of the bodies were so badly burned they were difficult to identify as human remains.

The Oakland Police Department provided a list of damage by street, but cautioned that "it may contain errors or omissions; house numbers may be inaccurate because house numbers have been obliterated."

The *Oakland Tribune* carried a story about a local policeman who toured the scene the day after the fire. He said, "It's just hell up there. I was in Vietnam and it looks just like places in Nam did after a napalm run."

CHAPTER NINE

DECISIONS

SOME PEOPLE MAKE SNAP DECISIONS AND DON'T look back. I've never been that kind of person. I've been known to walk out of a supermarket when I can't decide which can of soup to buy. I've spent thirty minutes choosing a pair of white socks. On really bad shopping days, having to make any decision—no matter how small—gets me flummoxed. But after the fire, decisions came up one after another and we didn't have time to procrastinate or second-guess.

Before we knew for sure about the fate of our house, before we were able to see for ourselves what happened, we talked about whether we would move or rebuild. If we had to rebuild, we decided we would rebuild on the same spot. We liked our neighborhood, and living across the street from the school had been ideal for us and for the kids. It didn't take us long to make up our minds. That decision was one of the easiest ones we had to make.

We called the contractor we'd worked with on our

kitchen remodeling job and set up a meeting. After that, we met and interviewed several architects before finding the right one.

We would be asked over and over again whether we were rebuilding, and it felt good to be able to say yes. It was the first step in our journey back home.

Although I dreaded the responsibility, I chose to take on the role of "project manager," which meant I would have to make decisions, both big and small, about everything every day—from doorknobs to wall finishes and trim, from appliances to carpeting. Once the rebuilding began, it would be my job to coordinate with the architect and general contractor. So I confessed early on to the architect that I might have a problem making decisions.

"You've got to help me," I begged. "This is going to be really hard for me."

He thought for a moment, and came up with a great idea. He suggested showing me only three options, and making some of the decisions himself.

"How about this: for the things that you will look at and touch every day, you make the choice. Leave the rest to me."

And that's how it worked. I did have to make plenty of decisions, but I got off the hook for door hinges and other small things. Neither of us cared to get bogged down with exotic tiles or light fixtures. He suggested paint colors, too, saving me from that slippery slope. I was lucky to work with an architect who figured out a way to get me past my paralysis in the face of decision making. As the construction progressed, I noticed that it got easier for me to make choices.

Breaking ground, June 3, 1992

Meanwhile, Bruce dealt with the insurance companies and red tape. And then there were the kids: the boys were still at Hillcrest together, but Caitlin attended middle school a couple of miles away. Instead of hopping on a bus or walking across the street, they each needed to be dropped off and picked up. Caitlin's basketball practice and Myles's tap lessons and rehearsals meant more trips back and forth. I'd never needed to carpool before, but it became a necessity when I couldn't be two places at once.

I had taken some time off after the fire but then went back

to my counseling job at the hospital. Bruce had to keep up with his practice as well as managing the back and forth with our insurance agents, making sure that we didn't leave anything out on our claims. On a typical morning, when the kids and I were running late, we'd take the back road that winds through Moraga and Canyon and ends up in Oakland's Montclair Village. I'd circle the block while two of the kids ran into Noah's and ordered bagels for their lunches. Many of those days felt frantic and disorganized, but I never forgot to pick anyone up. On the days when I drove west through the tunnel that bores through the hills to Oakland, the sight of the bridges and the bay brought tears to my eyes. I wanted to be home again so desperately.

------------------------- ARTIFACT -------------------------

🔥

CAT BLANKET

A FRIEND OF MINE MADE US A QUILT AS A BABY GIFT FOR Myles, inspired by a picture she'd seen on a greeting card: an appliquéd family portrait of two cats and three kittens, curled up together on a plaid blanket beneath a window full of stars. Myles called it his cat blanket.

As we evacuated the house on the day of the fire, James grabbed the pale-yellow quilt from his bed. He also took his favorite stuffed toy: the little fuzzy snowman. He'd be able to sleep peacefully anywhere with the familiar yellow quilt held next to his face and the snowman by his side. But in my haste to grab a few necessities from around the house, I had over-looked the blanket on Myles's bed.

It's the one thing he talked about often after the fire— wishing he'd brought it with him, even though he didn't get the chance to make the choice. He liked the way he used to be able to wiggle his fingers under the frayed edges of the fabric around the windows.

Myles didn't ask about the cat blanket when he hopped into the car to evacuate, but with swirling smoke and ash bearing down by then, would we have gone back for it? I like to think I would have, but he didn't ask about it until that first disjointed bedtime, when it was much too late.

Why didn't I think to grab the blanket as I went through

the house? What would have provided greater comfort to a child who got uprooted the way he did than the familiar feel of flannel at bedtime?

One day when James was around three, I had taken a series of photos of the boys featuring James lying under the blanket in a number of locations all over the house, including on top of the washer and dryer.

That blanket was like a member of the family.

We all missed it.

After we settled into the rental house and got the kids set up in their own rooms, I hatched a plan to recreate the cat blanket. Myles missed his anchor to his past, and I wanted—no, needed—to help him reconnect with it. We couldn't go back and make things exactly the way they were, but I figured maybe replacing the blanket was a good place to start.

Together Myles and I pored over the photo albums we had brought with us from the house and found enough pictures of the blanket to remind us exactly how it looked. I took him along with me to fabric stores all over the East Bay with a list of essential elements to gather: we needed mint-green and pale-yellow flannel for the background and border, just the right sort of brown plaid—with a touch of yellow and red—for the kitties' blanket; carnation-pink velveteen for one cat and one kitten; a mint-green velveteen for one of the kittens, and a midnight-blue satin sprinkled with tiny white stars for the night sky outside the cats' window. Checking the pictures for accuracy, we searched through bolts of corduroy to find the right coppery-brown color to use for the other cat and kitten, and for the frames around the windows filled with stars. Finally, we bought a small amount of white satin for the crescent moon that would smile down on the cat family.

I enlisted two talented friends—one who could draw and one who made quilts—to recreate the blanket. The whole project took two months to finish, from gathering the fabric, to the design work, to the appliquéing and quilting. Like many things we were able to replace, the cat blanket served as a reminder that close enough will never be the real thing—but it can still be good.

Shortly after my friends completed the quilt and presented it to him, around six months after the fire, Myles reported that the seams around the windows had started to unravel, just where they had unraveled on the original blanket. That familiar weakness turned out to be the best thing about the replacement.

---------- ARTIFACT ----------

ORANGE T-SHIRT

THE SHIRT WAS A GAG GIFT FROM A FRIEND, RECEIVED sometime in 1980 after Myles was born. Bright orange, like the candy wrapper that inspired it, the shirt read "Reese's Peanut Butter Cups—Two Great Tastes!" in big brown letters across the front. This was back when I might actually wear a T-shirt with something written on it—even one with a double meaning, since I was nursing a baby at the time. T-shirts, jeans, and bare feet—my mom-at-home uniform in those days.

I was wearing my orange shirt on the afternoon of my tenth wedding anniversary, watching Caitlin while she played in front of the house. She took off running down the street, even though she'd been told a million times not to. We lived on a steep hill, and I worried that she would stumble and fall. I watched with horror as she did just that—tumbling head over heels like Jack and Jill until she rolled to a stop in a neighbor's flower bed. I raced after her, my heart pounding, certain that she had broken something, everything, would need stitches, surgery, traction. All I found was a little cut on her chin, but it bled profusely all over my Reese's Peanut Butter Cups—Two Great Tastes T-shirt as I picked her up and hugged her. When we got back to the house, I took her to the emergency room while Bruce stayed home with our toddler son.

We waited to be seen at the hospital for what seemed like hours while she shook and sniffled, and I tried not to think about how much worse things could have been. And as we sat there, listening to crying babies and whining children, and breathing in that unmistakably stale antiseptic hospital smell, I couldn't help thinking about how I'd spent four months at Caitlin's bedside when she was a baby, while she recovered from open-heart surgery. Her recovery was complicated and slow, with some very low points along the way. On a particularly bad day, one of our nurses took me aside and said, "Your husband is your best bet right now." I looked at her for a long moment while the gravity of what she said sunk in. We knew our baby was in bad shape, but we never allowed ourselves to imagine the worst. And there it was suddenly: a possibility. I think this well-meaning nurse was trying to prepare me to face my greatest fear—that nothing the doctors could do would save her. Bruce and I would have to discuss the what-ifs . . . and we'd need to be strong for each other. But soon after my conversation with the nurse, Caitlin turned a corner and her condition slowly improved.

Once we got her home, we tried not to treat Caitlin like a sick kid. And she wasn't a sick kid. She made up for lost time as she learned to roll over and crawl. I'd hoped that she would have a fresh start, and would cruise through her childhood with nothing more than an occasional "owie" that I could kiss and make better. But you just can't protect your child every minute.

For our anniversary that year, we'd reserved a room at the Claremont Hotel, had arranged for the kids to be taken care of for the night, and booked a dinner reservation at a white-tablecloth restaurant nearby. This was a big deal—ten years. The high school sweethearts, now parents of two, things going well —let's celebrate, we thought. Then the transmission went out on our car, and we had to change our plans. The transmission cost as much as our big weekend would have, and we couldn't afford both. No matter what Hallmark says, for us the tenth anniversary was not wood or paper or whatever: it was the emergency room in a bloody T-shirt and a new transmission.

My daughter didn't need any stitches, nothing was broken or even sprained, and when we came home that night, I was too exhausted to care about celebrating. I couldn't stop thinking about the way her body twisted and picked up momentum as she rolled down the hill. I changed out of the bloody shirt, hoping the stains wouldn't be permanent.

That night, after we put the kids to bed, we had a quiet dinner at home and gamely toasted each other.

I NOW OWN TWO REESE'S PIECES T-SHIRTS, GIFTS FROM my kids. Truthfully, I haven't found an occasion to wear them in years, but I can't part with them either. They are reminders of the halcyon days of T-shirts, jeans, and bare feet—and of the way things can turn in an instant.

ARTIFACT

TREE HOUSE

WE HAD A HUGE MONTEREY PINE IN THE BACKYARD THAT had always called out for a tree house. The trunk was too big and its branches too high to climb, but the tree's position at the top of our uphill yard would make it an ideal crow's nest, a place to hide out with a book and a sandwich.

We decided to build a tree house in the summer of 1987, four years before the fire. A builder friend sketched out plans on a piece of paper. My friend the structural engineer vetted them, so our tree house was going to be well planned and solid. Bruce scoped out the lumberyard and loaded up the car with two-by-fours, dowels, and the necessary nails and bolts.

He built it in the evenings after work. The kids kept a close eye on the construction as the tree house gradually took shape. Everyone had an idea to contribute: James wanted a flag, so I bought a flag holder that we installed on the wooden railing. We flew a four-leafed clover flag for luck, and we raised the Stars and Stripes on the Fourth of July. Caitlin painted "Tree House Sweet Tree House" on a wooden plaque that we mounted next to the flag. We strung a rainbow-colored wind sock from the lower edge, and Myles came up with the idea of rigging a bucket on a rope for hoisting supplies.

The tree house turned out to be the perfect place for a family picnic or a quiet read. You had to go all the way to the top of the slope in the backyard to reach the back side of the tree, which is where the wooden ladder led up to the platform. Two-and-a-half-year-old James was not allowed to climb up by himself because it made me nervous.

One summer afternoon while washing dishes, I looked up and realized I'd lost sight of little James, who'd been playing in the backyard. Then I heard his voice, triumphantly announcing, "I'm up the tree house!" I could see the big tree through the kitchen window in front of me. He'd climbed up by himself, and his chest was puffed out proud.

"Don't move!" I yelled, and hurried outside. I raced up the path and climbed the rungs to join him.

"I'm up the tree house," he repeated softly.

Proud of him, but scared too, I gave him a hug, and we sat there together for a while. I wasn't ready for him to take such a big step by himself. I knew I wouldn't always be able to protect him and keep him out of harm's way, but I didn't want to think about that yet; I just wanted to hold him close.

After the fire, the scorched Monterey pine was tagged for removal. No trace of the tree house remained.

--- ARTIFACT ---

🔥

I'M TERRIFIC BECAUSE ...

MY SON MYLES WAS DANCING EVEN BEFORE HE WAS born. I used to lie in bed and watch as he shook his booty, creating amniotic tsunamis in my belly. On the night he made his first appearance, December 5, 1980, the nurse laid him on my stomach, and all at once my suspicions were confirmed—he was a boogying baby from day one.

When Myles was in second grade, his fabulous teacher asked every student to finish this sentence: "I'm terrific because . . ." and then draw a self-portrait to illustrate whatever sterling feature of their character they chose to highlight.

Myles drew a picture of a smiling boy with yellow hair, clad in a tuxedo, dancing on stage in front of a row of footlights, with the caption: I'm terrific because I can tap dance like Fred Astaire!

Myles idolized Donald O'Connor, Gene Kelly, and Savion Glover, back in his early Sesame Street days. We started looking in earnest for a place to get tap lessons when he was seven. He had been begging for them once he realized that his feet could make noise with the right shoes on. Myles had already choreographed his own dance at the school talent show, dressed in black and white with a red bow tie, wearing high-top sneakers and a sparkly silver derby.

So we began our search for the right place to learn the

waltz clog, the time step, and the shuffle off to Buffalo. There is no shortage of dance studios in the Bay Area, but the search was difficult just the same. Time after time, we would show up during a lesson and survey the teacher, the class, and the studio. No boys. Lots of sequins. Pictures sometimes lined the walls: rows of pretty girls in high-heeled tap shoes with high-cut leotards, more sequins, and still no boys. We moved on to the next place.

We finally found a home at a studio in Berkeley. Myles visited the class, which had several boys—some his age and some older—and danced across the wooden floor in his Converse high-tops. The teacher had a big smile and a loud voice, a head full of ringlets, and mismatched earrings. The kids danced to brassy show-biz tunes that got their feet moving. The pictures on the walls were of tap legends: Sandman Sims, Gregory Hines, the Nicholas Brothers, and others. Not a sequin in sight. When the class ended and the kids tumbled out the door, I noticed that my son had a new look on his face: his eyes were shining and his smile was one of joy mixed with gratitude—a wish fulfilled. We signed him up for the class and hurried off to buy his first pair of shiny black tap shoes.

When Myles was around ten, we attended a Jazz Tap Summit in San Francisco, where all the living legends of tap performed and spoke to a sold-out crowd of tappers and wannabes. The audience was encouraged to "bring your shoes" and join in at the end for a big jam session. Naturally, Myles laced up and ran onstage with all the others. It was a huge thrill to see him on the stage doing the shim sham shimmy with all the big-time tappers. When he returned to our seats, he said, "Sandman Sims talked to me!"

"What did he say?" we asked. Proud parents that we were, we waited for some comment on his innate ability, his sense of rhythm, or his poise as a performer.

"He said, 'Go this way.' And then he said, 'Now go that way.'" Myles was beaming.

My son had many wonderful experiences with his tap shoes on, all the way through high school, college, and beyond —including a jam session where he traded steps with Gregory Hines. Myles is in his thirties now and bears little resemblance to that blonde boy with the bow tie. He's still dancing, though, every chance he gets.

He may not be able to dance quite like Fred Astaire, but he certainly looked like him—complete with white-tie, tails, and top hat—at his wedding several years ago. As we waited to walk down the aisle, he struck a pose and asked me, "Was I not born to wear this outfit?"

And I had to say yes, he definitely was. I told him, "You look terrific."

The day of the fire I didn't think to take his "I'm terrific" picture, but I can still see it: the happy boy with the black bow tie, dancing with his feet off the ground.

CHAPTER TEN

THE HOUSE WITH THE PHONE BOOTH

After a few days of frantic searching in Moraga, we found a house to rent: ranch-style, four bedrooms, two baths, big kitchen/dining area, nasty green shag carpet, untended backyard—but plenty of room. The one unique feature of the house was a phone booth down the hall just past the first bedroom. Just a tiny cubicle, about the size of the old-fashioned phone booths that used to be on every street corner. A little bench angled in one corner provided a place to sit, and a bifold door provided a measure of privacy. The address of the house had the number fourteen in it—a good omen, since Bruce and I and our daughter were born on the fourteenth of June, November, and December, respectively. That sealed the deal, and we signed a lease on the spot. We saw other cars pulling up to the house as we left and felt relieved to have made this one big decision.

The next step was to rent furniture. We found a showroom in Oakland where we could rent couches, dressers, chairs, and tables—everything we needed—on short notice and have them delivered to the rental house.

Friends offered to help us move.

"Do you have room in your car for a paper bag?" I asked them. My attempt at humor. I appreciated the sentiment, but we had plenty of room in our cars for the photo albums and the few brown shopping bags full of hand-me-downs that had poured in almost immediately. It was by far the easiest move we ever made.

FEMA and the Red Cross pitched in to make our transitions go smoothly. We got vouchers for food and coupons for stores. For permits and information, FEMA set up an efficient one-stop shop in an empty building within a month after the fire. The local Catholic school set up tables piled with clothes and toys, and invited fire survivors to take whatever we needed. We went, and saw people from the neighborhood filling baskets with T-shirts, skirts, jackets, and sweaters. Bruce and I found clothes for work, and the kids found school clothes and jackets.

Our neighborhood has three schools within as many blocks of each other. The school the boys attended had 236 students; fifty families lost their homes in the fire. We heard later that the firefighters set up a line in the street, in front of the houses on my block, in order to protect the schools. Someone filmed them standing with their backs against the chain link fence at the edge of the school yard, hoses aimed at our houses, trying to contain the flames and stop them from spreading across the street or down the block where the schools were located. I saw this film once, and I've tried to block the images from my memory.

I couldn't argue with the fire fighters' decision to save the schools. Our school became an anchor for the dispossessed families. Friends and neighbors used our school as a meeting place, and volunteers rallied to provide meals and support for all the fire survivors. Counselors came and talked to the kids and held meetings for the parents to help us deal with the blame and the anger the kids felt toward the city, their parents, the firefighters—and the universe—for turning their world upside down.

Macy's, Penney's, and other stores gave generous discounts to folks like us who were starting households from scratch. They also set up a registry, like a bridal registry, so we could list our needs. We filled huge shopping bags at the stores: pillows, sheets, towels, blankets, shoes. During one of these shopping trips, Caitlin decided to cheer her father up with a gift. "I'll be right back," she told us, and walked down the aisle toward the men's department. A few minutes later, she returned with a bag and handed it to Bruce. He reached in and pulled out an aloha shirt: a cheerful red one, covered with blue-and-yellow orchids and green palm fronds. Caitlin had used her allowance to replace the kind of shirt that she knew would remind her dad of happier times on an island beach.

My wonderful friends—Jo, Sara, Janiele, Cindy, Lisa, Jan, and Peggy—threw a surprise shower for Chris and me: laundry baskets full of household items and necessities. We received a gift certificate for a children's bookstore so we could replace our read-aloud favorites. Bruce got choked up when he took the three kids to replace our copies of *Madeline*, *Winnie the Pooh*, and *The Giving Tree*, among others.

In preparation for our move, we'd ordered beds: two twins, a double, and a king. But they didn't arrive until the day after we moved in, so the first night in the rental house we camped out on the floor with our new pillows and comforters. We hadn't had time to launder anything first; the sheets were stiff and creased, and the strange scent of their plastic casings clung to them.

After a couple of washings with our familiar detergent, our new bedding and towels felt like our own. It was a start.

How would we make this place feel like home? Every home has its own look, feel, and smell. How would we recreate that, when we'd done it without thinking before? The questions we asked ourselves were: How do you create a home from scratch? What defines home? If things don't matter—and you don't have things anyway—what makes the place we live more than just a house? For the sake of our children, we had to figure this out.

We'd already taken care of the basics: beds, a place to gather for meals, books for bedtime reading, and music. Bruce bought a turntable and speakers and went to a music store to replace his favorite records.

"I miss my friends," he told the guy behind the counter. He came home with stacks of albums. Once again he could listen to his beloved jazz, blues, and rock 'n' roll.

And I went to the yarn store. My first knitting project after the fire was a purple vest that I would finish but never wear. I just needed to get something going, to hear the needles sliding against each other and feel the yarn in my hands. I'd learned to knit while I was in high school, and every sweater I'd ever made—several for my husband and for each of the kids —was gone, along with the box full of baby sweaters and blankets I'd tucked away, just in case we might have grand-children eventually.

Almost every day we'd come up short when we needed something: tape, scissors, Band-Aids, paper towels, big spoons, notepads, pens, cleaning supplies, or sandwich bags. Or a needle and thread, cinnamon, mustard, olive oil, aluminum foil, a spatula. One night right after we moved in, some red wine spilled on the rug. We realized that we couldn't do our stan-dard cleanup method—salt to absorb it, then vacuuming—and had to go buy both salt and a vacuum cleaner the next day.

Bruce had grabbed our big black binder with the recipes in it when he left the house the day of the fire, so once we got the kitchen pulled together we could make our famous spa-ghetti again. We'd served many of our friends that spaghetti over the years since college. (We had once taken out an ad and sold the World Famous Spaghetti recipe for $1.00. We made five bucks). The binder contained recipes we'd been collecting since we got married, and I marveled that he'd thought to take it. The binder held the kids' favorite chocolate chip cookie recipe, as well as the formula for the boozy Tom and Jerry drinks that were a Christmas Eve tradition for the grownups. It chronicled everything, from the multicourse dinners we prepared in the years BC (before children), to the ambitious goodies like truffles and babas au rhum we used to give as gifts and the big family-size casseroles we favored more recently.

Neither of us really felt like cooking at first. For one thing, we lacked the necessary equipment to do anything more complicated than microwaving. Until we had pots, pans, and more time and energy, cooking slid way down on the priority list. We relied on takeout and the kindness of others for many days. The local pizza place got to know our order by heart. But when we did get around to cooking finally, the pot of spaghetti sauce filled the house with a familiar aroma.

One night the kids and I went to visit friends. While we were out, Bruce killed off a bottle of wine. I came home and found him already in bed, feeling sorry for himself, sorry for all of us. Later that night as he moaned and complained about how terrible he felt, I wasn't very sympathetic. In fact, I was pretty steamed. I complained about it to my friend Carol on the phone the next day. "A whole bottle of wine!" I said. "As if that was going to make anything better." Carol heard me out, then quietly urged me to calm down. "It's understandable," she said. "Let it go."

I tried to stay organized and focused, without looking back too much, but when I was alone I wept and screamed— usually while driving. And there were meltdowns, like the one in the shoe store. We'd lost all our checks, and we couldn't order new ones until we had a permanent address. In the meantime, most businesses would accept a deposit slip made out and signed like a check. I'd done this many times and never had a problem. If a salesclerk asked me about it, I just explained about the fire. It was never an issue. Except for the time in the shoe store. The sulky clerk wouldn't take my temporary check. "It's been over a month. You should've taken care of this by now," she said. In response, I pitched the pair of shoes across the counter, and swore at her over my shoulder as I ran to my car.

One day when the kids weren't being cooperative I stormed out of the house, leaving three crying kids inside—something I promised myself I would never do. Walking out on us was one of the things my mother did when she was angry with me and my sister, and I thought it was inexcusable and one of the worst things a mother could do. But I did it anyway: grabbed my keys and slammed the door on my way out.

I called Bruce from a phone booth outside the coffee shop where I'd fled and told him tearfully that I'd left the kids but would definitely go back in and get them, and was I really a terrible mother?

Incidents like this, barely six weeks after the fire, forced us to realize that the stress was getting to us. I hardly slept and found myself experiencing short-term memory loss, which is my go-to stress reaction. I remembered feeling the same way after Caitlin was born. We felt overscheduled and overwhelmed. I worried that something important would fall through the cracks and get overlooked. Out of necessity, with three kids and too many things to do, we instituted what became a dreaded Sunday-night ritual: the calendar conference.

Bruce, the two older kids, and I pulled out our calendars and made notes for the week: who had a late practice or rehearsal, who would cook dinner on what nights, and when would we take the easy way out and get pizza or takeout. We learned about a place just a few blocks away that sold a variety of pasta and sauces, along with salad and a loaf of bread, which became our fallback dinner plan. The local pizza place delivered on those nights when we didn't feel like going to pick it up ourselves. With only two drivers in the family, we had to orchestrate our trips back and forth from Moraga to Oakland, a distance of just over eight miles each way. We never stranded a kid and only once messed up the carpool during that time.

As we began the rebuilding process, I spent most of my time in the car going from one appointment to the next. Some days I felt like all I did was drive around, hoping to have a few moments in a place that had a bathroom and a telephone, before I moved on to the next meeting. My friends would understand when I asked if I could come over and make use of their facilities. My most basic needs boiled down to finding a phone and a place to pee.

ARTIFACT

🔥

PINK DRESS

IF A TRAVEL AGENT HADN'T MESSED UP OUR RESERVATION and nearly left us without a hotel room in New York that time, I never would have found the pink dress in an upscale beach town's secondhand store. As an apology for his mistake, and for our embarrassment at the check-in desk at a hotel that had never heard of us or our reservation, the travel agent comped us to a weekend stay at the Ritz Carleton in Laguna Niguel.

We tore ourselves away from the luxurious seaside resort one afternoon to wander through the nearby town. I'd spotted a secondhand shop on our way to the hotel and thought I might be able to find something to wear to the fancy wedding we'd been invited to that winter. "What I'm looking for," I explained to Bruce, "is something someone wore to the Oscars and then gave away." And once I got inside the store, I found exactly what I was looking for: a glittery rack crammed with drop-dead beautiful dresses that looked as though they'd been down a red carpet at least once. I had found the mother lode of cast-off couture.

I tried on a mermaid dress with a tail, a red sequined number, a champagne satin pleated and draped disaster . . . and then I saw the pink dress. Silk chiffon in ballerina pink, just a whisper of color, with a handkerchief hem, dropped waist banded in pink satin, and sheer sleeves with the same pink satin at the cuffs. A light sprinkling of rhinestones on the bodice added a touch of bling. It was love at first sight. Just one problem: it was two sizes too big. But I bought it anyway, figuring I could get it altered in plenty of time for the wedding.

Once we got home, I took the dress to a nearby bridal shop. I was sure they could cut the dress down and shorten the sleeves for me. I tried it on in front of a seamstress who wore glasses on a chain and a pincushion on her wrist. She marked the dress, pinned it, pulled it in, and showed me what she would do to make it fit.

A week later, I went back to the shop and twirled in front of the mirror in my pink dress. Perfect! Sleeves, length, bodice —as if it had been made for me in the first place.

I found some pewter shoes—not too flashy—just barely silver, the color of the rhinestones when they reflected light.

Oh, that perfect, lovely pink dress. I wore it twice, once to the wedding and once to a New Year's Eve party. We posed for a picture at the house before we left for the wedding but hadn't yet taken the film to be developed. I grabbed a roll of undeveloped film when we left the house ahead of the fire, and that's why I have a picture of the pink dress.

I held onto that roll of film for months. Getting it developed slipped way down on the priority list. But when I finally took it in and got the pictures back, I gasped with joy. A long lost friend, missing and presumed gone forever—found!

We are in prom-picture formation: Bruce has his arm around me; our hands are joined in front of us. He looks sharp in his tuxedo, bow tie, and crisp white shirt. My hair is up, my silvery earrings sparkle, and the light catches in the soft folds of the pink satin.

The pink dress: diaphanous, ethereal, light as a pair of fairy wings.

—————————— ARTIFACT ——————————

🔥

R E D   S H O E S

THEY WERE FIRE-ENGINE RED. CHERRIES IN THE SNOW red; million-dollar red; movie star pouty lips, just like on *Mad Men* red. An I-mean-business red. They had a high heel with narrow patent leather and suede strips arched diagonally across the toe. Sexy and fun to wear: my kind of shoe. I had two red dresses and a red straw hat. Red from head to toe.

I loved those shoes. Eventually, because of a few scuffs they acquired at parties and weddings, the shoes needed polishing. I like to polish shoes and probably don't do it often enough. I learned from my dad but may not have been paying really close attention. I bought some red shoe polish, and after scanning the directions on the little jar, I applied the polish and let it dry.

Big mistake.

Nasty-looking streaks of dark red defaced my once-glorious shoes. They looked horrible. I was determined to save them. I had to take action.

My next step was to take my streaky, smeared, no longer fabulous-looking shoes to a repair shop, with the hope that a professional shoe person could restore them to their former flashy glory. "Sure," the guy said. "I can re-dye them and they will look like new. No problem." I left my shoes and awaited their rebirth the following week.

I returned to the repair shop, fished out my ticket, and reclaimed my shoes. What I saw made my jaw drop. The dull, tomato soup-colored shoes he handed me were listless and pathetic, the life and sparkle painted right out of them. My once-ruby slippers belonged back in Kansas. I took them home, like sick kittens huddled in a box.

Now, I am not one of those women who hide price tags and pretend that new clothes are old to fool their husbands. I had spent a fair amount of money on the red shoes, a fact I am sure I mentioned to Bruce, but maybe not. What I did next was underhanded, sneaky, and motivated by pure vanity: I took money from our savings account, drove back to the store, and bought the shoes again. I quietly disposed of the dreadful dyed pair, and never mentioned the switch. Why would I? My shoes and I were back in the swing at parties and dinners and weddings. In between events, they had a place of honor in my closet. Just seeing them every day gave me a lift.

I hadn't counted on losing them again.

THE WAY I REMEMBER IT, BRUCE AND I WERE DRIVING through Oakland on the way back to his parents' house when I told him about the shoes. This was a couple of days after we knew the house was gone. While we like to tell stories now about our first reactions, the ones that sound lighthearted and optimistic ("We finally got rid of the junipers out front," or "We'll rebuild and get bigger closets"), and it's true, we said those things to each other, but it's also true we said other things you don't say often enough when life is going along just fine, like: "I love you so much"; "I know I can always depend on you"; "You're being so strong for all of us"; "We'll make it through this"; and "We hold each other up, we always have."

And as we drove past the blackened hills of what used to be our neighborhood, I confessed through gulping sobs that I had bought a second pair of red shoes with money I had spirited out of our savings account. It hardly mattered at that point, but I told him anyway. I was sorry for my carelessness, sorry for the deception, sorry for such vanity, sorry for all of it.

ONE OF MY FRIENDS, KNOWING THE EXTENT OF OUR LOSS from the fire, expressed her sympathy and then cried out, "Your shoes!" I know, I know. I had lots of great shoes. All gone. I tried to keep things in perspective: we survived, we could start over, it could have been so much worse. Who thinks to grab red shoes when she's running from a firestorm? It didn't even enter my mind.

Those red shoes belong to another lifetime. Even if I could still find them, would I buy them again? I will admit to being superstitious: what if the third time was not the charm? Would I spend the rest of my life sniffing the air for smoke?

CHAPTER ELEVEN

A SAD HALLOWEEN

October 31

Halloween came less than two weeks after the fire, and we were still settling into our rental house. To my young children, Halloween was by far the most important day of the year. Normally, I would help research, design, and fabricate homemade costumes for the kids. As the family photographer, I went to every Halloween parade and kept a record of all the crazy costumes my kids roped me into making for them. I sewed, stayed up late for several nights, and created some fine costumes for those kids. One year, I had transformed Caitlin into Miss Liberty, swathed in green fabric, with a flashlight lamp for her to hold up, topped off with the foam crown I'd purchased from a New York vendor months in advance. She'd also been a colorful hippie, and a sassy waitress. One year Myles was a mad scientist, with hazmat tape, a white lab coat, and a tube of glow-in-the-dark goo.

But Halloween 1991 turned out to be a low-key event.

The only picture I have from that day is of James, dressed as Waldo, wearing a red watch cap and parts of his Waldo pj's. Not up to the usual standards, but there just wasn't time, energy, or incentive to be more creative.

Because our house had been across from the school yard, if I could find a place to stand at the edge of the Halloween parade facing east, our house would always be in the background.

Its red brick facade below the blue clapboard stood out from the light-colored houses on the block. But after the fire, there were no houses across the street from school. Standing in my same spot that year on Halloween, all I could see were empty lots, foundations, and chimneys.

Back in our house in Moraga that night, we'd seriously underestimated the amount of candy we'd be handing out to trick-or-treaters. We had bought several bags, but we ran out early. Since we'd left the lights on, a group of hopeful kids rang our doorbell again. A small gaggle of goblins stood on our porch and sang out, "Trick or treat!"

I told them I wasn't trying to trick them, but we had no more candy.

"We just moved here from Oakland," I said. "We're not used to so many trick-or-treaters."

"Oh, that's okay," one of the kids said, and then he pulled out handfuls of loot from his bag and told the others to do the same. We refilled the bowl, thanked the kids, and were able to answer the door for the next several groups.

---------- ARTIFACT ----------

🔥

KING KONG

MANY PEOPLE HAVE LOVELY ANGEL ORNAMENTS TO TOP their Christmas trees. Not my family. We have King Kong.

Four years into our marriage, I finally let my husband talk me into getting a tree of our own. I had my reasons for resisting. We had three cats, we lived in a small apartment, and since I grew up in a Jewish family, I was not accustomed to having a tree in my living room for weeks at a time. He wore me down, though, and when I relented at last, he dashed out the door promising to bring home a beautiful tree and protect it with a cat-proof barrier that he would make himself.

"Not too big?" I pleaded, as he raced out.

"Right!" he answered, as excited as, well, a kid on Christmas morning.

"And ornaments?" I yelled after him.

"Sure thing!" he said.

Because my mother-in-law used to transform the family home into a jolly red-and-white winter wonderland with Santas and reindeer on every possible horizontal surface every December, I trusted that her son would have the know-how to choose appropriate ornaments with which to decorate our first tree. I awaited his return, surprisingly eager to begin a new tradition with special ornaments that we would hand down to the children we might have some day. I imagined he would bring home shiny round ornaments in silver and gold, and maybe some garlands that we would drape over the branches. Little reindeer? Santas? I guessed he would choose things that were traditional, but maybe a bit fun, too. I was getting into it.

He came back some time later with a lovely and not-too-big tree, some lumber and hinges, and a few other things. But oh, those other things!

I'm still not sure why, but he had visited the local toy store and come back with a big bag full of the ugliest plastic animals I had ever seen. I'm talking about dinosaurs and water buffalo and pigs and giraffes—each one more hideous than the last. Among these badly painted monstrosities was a rubber ape, with one arm raised menacingly over his head.

"What were you thinking, exactly?" I asked him when he proudly presented his sorry collection of would-be ornaments. I guess he may have thought something at the time, but wisely decided to keep it to himself. Instead, we both went to the store and bought a string of lights, bags of cranberries, popcorn, tinsel, and a few more traditional ornaments. I spent a delightful afternoon stringing the popcorn and cranberries, and placing strands of tinsel and ornaments just so on the "not too big, is it?" tree. We got rid of the ugly plastic animals, but kept the rubber ape and gave him the place of honor atop the tree. The cats kept a close eye on the whole process, tails and ears twitching.

The next year, we got a slightly bigger tree and added a few more ornaments. And we had our first baby. In the years that followed, we got more ornaments, had more babies, and bought bigger trees.

Once they got old enough to ask, "Where did King Kong

come from?" we took each of our three children aside and explained the tradition. To their credit, they accepted the fact that their parents were a little goofy and let it go at that. They all helped decorate the tree every December as we hung their handmade ornaments along with the ones we accumulated over the years. The big moment always came when Dad got up on the stepstool and placed King Kong at the very top.

THAT FIRST HOLIDAY SEASON AFTER THE FIRE, WE HAD TO scramble. We realized that there was no way to replace fifteen years' worth of acquired Christmas decorations and ornaments. Some were just plain irreplaceable, but others . . .

With fingers crossed, we drove back to the toy store where Old King Kong came from to see if we could find a replacement for him. What joy we felt when we spied the menacing little fellow in a bin full of other beasts! We purchased the new guy, along with a few reindeer, and brought them back to our temporary home, where we had a subdued Christmas in the still-unfamiliar house.

We put up the tree and hung the new ornaments, including a small house made of clay with the inscription: Next year in Oakland. The kids gathered around as their dad put King Kong in his rightful place at the top of the tree. That ugly rubber tree topper made us feel as though we were somehow on the way back to normal. And I remember curling up on the couch, watching the family together, feeling a little bit like the cats on Myles's blanket: like the old us, but different. Us in a new place, but still us, together under the stars.

ARTIFACT

🔥

ROTISSERARY

WHEN WE WERE FIRST MARRIED, BRUCE AND I LIVED IN A
WWII-era fourplex on a busy corner in Albany, California—a
small city next door to Berkeley. For four and a half years we
lived in the bottom apartment on the left in the white
clapboard house with green shutters. We managed to coexist
with three indoor cats in that compact space. Friends and
family squeezed into our place for noisy parties and elaborate
meals.

Our half-size apartment stove competed for space in the
kitchen with the water heater, the refrigerator, and place
settings for the cats. In our dollhouse kitchen, all movements
had to be carefully choreographed so we could work together.
We perfected the do-si-do maneuver necessary to pass from
the corner sink to the stove as we chopped, washed, or stirred.
The biggest and least practical horizontal surface in the
kitchen was the deep triangular shelf that reached back from
the tiled backsplash. A macramé plant holder, containing a
spindly specimen reaching toward the only window, hung
from a hook in the ceiling over the shelf.

We started cooking together in high school and continued
to feed our friends all the way through college and his three
years of law school. We'd make big pots of chili and pans of
cornbread for our post-football-game parties, and actually used

our Crock-Pot—a standard-issue wedding present in the '70s. Another house specialty in those days: our famous spaghetti, always accompanied by crunchy garlic bread and lots of jug red.

We experimented with Chinese dishes, using a Time Life book (another wedding present). I made wonton soup from scratch, chopping by hand in those pre-food-processor days the pork, ginger, and spinach for the filling, folding the wrappers, sealing them quickly and dropping the little packets into homemade chicken broth. Our big wok, a gift we had actually asked for, barely fit on the stovetop, but we used it to stir fry a variety of dishes.

Our menus grew in scope and level of difficulty, and we sought new challenges. Why not try Peking duck with Mandarin pancakes, scallion brushes, and hoisin sauce—the whole deal? We bought a fresh duck, then read step one of the recipe, which directed us to "loop a length of white cord under the wings," and then "suspend the bird from the string in a cool, airy place for three hours to dry the skin, or train a fan on it for two hours." Exploring our options for this part of the process, we took down the plant and hung up the duck.

We dragged out our electric rotisserie, a wedding present from a great-aunt (who pronounced it "rotisserary"), and placed it on the shelf above the sink, directly underneath the dangling duck. We figured that the heating element of the rotisserie would serve as a good substitute for a fan while hastening the drying process. But as soon as we plugged it in, it blew a fuse, which meant we had to unplug whatever else was plugged in for the duration of the drying-out period. Plug in, blow fuse, repeat.

Meanwhile, juices from the duck hit the red-hot heating element below, producing a sizzling siren song for the cats. The three of them—Catrina, the calico with the crooked tail; Midnight, the skittish longhaired black cat; and sleek, gray Kinky Raoul—lined up and posed like ancient stone cats, their eyes glued to the flightless indoor bird. Six eyes narrowed to slits; an occasional ear twitched. If that duck made a move, I am sure they would have jumped straight up in the air like cartoon cats.

After a couple of hours, the hapless duck was liberated from its noose and plunged into a boiling concoction of water, honey, gingerroot, and scallions. The cats used this reprieve to huddle together. I imagined them pooling their knowledge in order to calculate the precise amount of thrust and velocity required to leap up and take a whack at the duck, should such an opportunity present itself.

Following its dip in the flavorful aromatic bath, the bird was strung up again to twist slowly in the window for another couple of hours. Eventually, the cats sensed the futility of their duck watch. One by one, they crept off to find a square of sunlight somewhere, to sleep and dream of indoor ducks, cooked and crispy, within their grasp.

Later that night, we enjoyed a lovely dinner. The cats, ever hopeful, brushed against our legs under the table.

WE KEPT THE ROTISSERIE IN THE GARAGE ALONG WITH the other rarely used kitchen equipment we had. No trace of it was found after the fire, and we never replaced it.

CHAPTER TWELVE

LIFE BEGINS AT FORTY

Less than a month after the fire, I celebrated my fortieth birthday. Bruce had planned a wonderful party for me, with a big band, caterers, flowers, and a huge cake with the inscription, "Who'd a thunk it?" which could have meant a lot of things. Who'd have thought we'd be forty? Who'd have thought we'd lose our house? Who'd have thought that two teenagers would stick together over the long haul? Who'd have thought we'd be in a mood to celebrate barely a month after facing a major life-changing event?

The party was to be held at a local facility that had a large room with a great dance floor and places for folks to sit. Bruce arranged it months before the fire. The invitations went out in early October, and he'd heard from many of the invited guests already. In early November, people started calling to see if the party was still on. "Of course," he told them. "If ever there was a time we needed to be with our friends and families . . ." When they asked what I needed, he answered, "That's easy—everything!"

And so people came out on a rainy night to see us and wish me a happy birthday. Friends and family twirled on the dance floor and posed for lots of pictures. The night flew by.

I wore a black dress with an overlay of sequins. I managed to dance in three-inch patent-leather heels. I look happy in the pictures—tired, but happy. Although I'd been dreading it, turning forty turned out to be the least of my problems that year. For one night, anyway, we danced and drank, embraced each other, and counted our blessings: good friends, family, resilience, and faith in our ability to come out of this stronger.

We didn't feel like victims; we felt like survivors. Victims lost their lives, or lost their way. We lost a home and our possessions, but we did not lose the strength we would need to carry on. We certainly had no idea what lay ahead of us in the coming year: all the frustration and patience involved in the process of rebuilding our home, all the ways we had to struggle to reclaim our lives, and the constant search for ways to get some "normal" back in our routines.

If I mourned the loss of "youth" on my fortieth birthday, it was more about losing the oldest things I had: special birthday cards; goofy letters from high school friends; my grandfather's magnificent penmanship, his letters written sometimes in four languages; an envelope containing autumn leaves from Vermont—a surprise from a friend during his freshman year of college. Sure, these were things I hadn't looked at in years, but I never forgot about them. There used to be an old saying: Life begins at forty—and in a way, it did. A new life began, anyway. It was the beginning of "after."

ARTIFACT

🔥

HAPPY TODAY PILLOW

MANY YEARS AGO, I FOUND THIS ODD LITTLE PILLOW IN Takahashi, an odd little store in San Francisco. The store carried an eclectic collection of items, and since it was on my way to work, I'd often poke my head inside to see what was new.

A friend was getting married, and I needed to buy him a gift. While browsing around the store one afternoon, I found the Happy Today pillow. Wide, oval shaped, and made of pale-yellow woven cotton, the pillow had two heads attached above and four legs below. The heads had yellow yarn hair, parted down the middle and stitched into waves; their delicate facial features were drawn in ink. With pink circles on the cheeks and mouths open in smiles, the faces appeared to be singing a joyful tune. Embroidered in red yarn in the oval's center—where you might expect bodies to join legs to heads— was the legend "Happy Today," which was surrounded by colorful stripes in orange, green, and blue yarn. Red yarn knots formed a border for the central message.

I picked up the pillow for a closer look; the four floppy legs dangled like little udders. The faces looked like young, happy likenesses of Bach. At least, they did to me. I was still holding the pillow when a clerk came over and stood next to me.

"It's one of a kind, that's for sure," he said.

"I know," I said. "Do you think this would make a good wedding present?"

He shrugged. "You seem to like it," he said. "Do you think the people you want to give it to would like it as much as you do?"

A tough call. If I'd received it as a wedding present, would I have liked it? Not practical, not fancy, not traditional. I was still a newlywed and had received some gifts that were hard to define. I would have liked it, I decided, but I wasn't sure about my friends.

So I left the store without the pillow.

But I came back the next day and went straight to the shelf where the pillow sat, resting its heads. The same clerk was there, watching me. He finally came over and said, "You know, no one else could possibly love this thing as much as you do. Why don't you buy them something else and get this for yourself?"

And that's what I did. I don't remember what I gave the newlyweds, but I got years of pleasure from looking at that silly pillow. I also don't remember how or why it ended up in James's room, but it must have been there because it's on the list that way.

———————————— ARTIFACT ————————————

🔥

GOLD WATCH

BRUCE'S GRANDFATHER LEFT HIM A GOLD WATCH; IT WAS thin and elegant, befitting a bank vice president, which his grandfather had been for many years. The watch remained in our safe deposit box during his teens and twenties. But when Bruce turned thirty and made partner at his law firm, he finally felt ready to wear the watch. And he did wear it for about ten years. Understated and just a little formal, the watch looked nice on his wrist. He kept it on top of his dresser every night. He didn't wear it on weekends, just to work.

He wasn't wearing the gold watch the day of the fire. And either he was too optimistic or he didn't think to grab it, but he left it behind on the dresser when he left the house.

Once we were allowed back on our block, he put on a pair of workman's overalls and heavy boots and planned to spend a couple of hours sifting through the ashes, hoping to find that watch. When he got there, he realized how hopeless it was. But still, he had to look. He stepped over bedsprings and bits of metal and concrete, sinking several inches into a mixture of ash and charred debris—the remains of our home. He left empty-handed, covered with ashes and soot.

We learned much later that the fire reached temperatures as high as 2,000 degrees Fahrenheit, hot enough to boil asphalt. Temperatures reached crematorium level. The watch would have melted.

CHAPTER THIRTEEN

THE HOLIDAYS

After my birthday in mid-November, we had to figure out what to do about Thanksgiving. We'd taken over the Thanksgiving family dinner years before, finally wresting it away from my father-in-law. As newlyweds, we went back and forth between our two families based on where the Cal/Stanford Big Game would be played: if in Berkeley, we'd spend it with Bruce's folks (his dad went to Cal); if at Stanford (my dad attended there) we'd be with mine.

And then, when the kids came along, it became easier for us to host both families, so that's what we did. The family grew, with new in-laws and the addition of four nephews. We gradually accumulated all the once-a-year things you need to accommodate large numbers of people: long white tablecloths, serving platters, carving boards, gravy boats and ladles, extra plates and napkins, a second set of flatware, place card holders, and so on. We had all that stuff. Bruce took on the cooking duties and I did setup, cleanup, cranberries, and flowers. The dinners may not have been as neatly or efficiently executed as his father's, but the food was good and plentiful.

Bruce inherited his father's love for hosting the annual feast, while I tried to come up with ways to tweak tradition. One year we had a Hawaiian-themed Thanksgiving, with the addition of some island-inspired ingredients, featuring pupu platters and pitchers of mai tais to get us started. Everyone showed up in aloha wear.

THE YEAR OF THE FIRE, WE HAD NEITHER THE TIME NOR the inclination to host a family dinner. And we lacked a fully equipped kitchen. So we returned to my in-laws' house, even though the football game was at Stanford that year. In the pictures from that first Thanksgiving we were all wearing new clothes. Though everyone smiled for the camera, they were half-smiles, brave smiles. We couldn't help remembering being at that table the night of the fire and several nights after that, and those were not good memories. When dinner was over, we drove home to Moraga. Next year we'll be back in Oakland, we told ourselves.

THE TWO OLDER KIDS HAVE BIRTHDAYS IN DECEMBER, nine days apart. We'd become veteran party-givers over the years, taking cues from the kids about how to plan. For her fourth birthday, Caitlin asked for a birthday band. We weren't sure what that meant exactly, but we provided kazoos, drums, and plastic horns, and borrowed a recording of John Philip

Souza marches from the library. The kids marched around the living room to the strains of "The Stars and Stripes Forever," while we laughed until we cried. Myles once requested a dress-up party, and all his little guests arrived suitably attired. He held court at the head of the table in a button-down shirt and bow tie. For James's first birthday, I made tuxedo bibs for his toddler guests: white pleated shirts with little red bow ties.

Myles invited his friends out to our house in Moraga for a mystery-themed party that first December. The parents were good sports, driving their kids over and picking them up a few hours later. We were still getting used to living there, and it felt a little strange to have kids over, when we'd had those same kids in our blue house many times before. They all liked the phone booth.

And then we had to deal with Hanukkah and Christmas. Most of the gifts we got the kids that year for birthdays and holidays were replacements for things they'd lost: bikes, toys, books, movies, and clothes. The "before" pictures of the Christmas tree feature piles of gifts; the "after" pictures show a living room full of torn paper and empty boxes, same as always.

We had our traditional Christmas breakfast after opening presents: French toast made from challah bread and eggnog. We all rode our new bikes afterward.

THAT YEAR OF FIRSTS—THANKSGIVING FOLLOWED BY birthdays and Christmas—found us reaching for the familiar and learning to recreate the rituals that had defined us as a family. Some of the old ways stuck, but some we had to let go. Each time we did something the way we used to before the fire, like starting a napkin fight at the dinner table, we felt one step closer to being home.

Still, our normal patterns were disrupted in the new surroundings.

We struggled to make the best of each holiday, but for some of them we just opted out. We'd hosted Passover seders for years, but I explained to my family that because I didn't feel especially passed over, I'd just as soon skip it.

ARTIFACT

🔥

BOXES

THE CEDAR BOX

I FOUND THE SMALL CEDAR BOX AT THE SAN JOSE FLEA market one hot summer afternoon. Bruce and I were spending the day with his college roommate, Tom, who lived nearby, and we decided to go check out the warrens of booths and tables spread out in the enormous parking lot. We weren't looking for anything in particular. It seemed like a harmless way to spend an hour or so after a night of beach camping and beer consumption. We were all around twenty then, still capable of sleeping on hard sand and waking up without achy bones.

The cedar box was on a table amidst a jumble of junk and old costume jewelry. The proprietor sat under a swag of faded fabric, watching the passing crowd with a bored expression. She barely looked up when I stopped to look closely at the little wooden box. A decoupage basket of flowers, slightly yellowed with age, covered the top. Both hinges worked, so I lifted the lid and peeked inside. No lining, just the unvarnished cedar. The box measured about ten inches across and six inches deep: big enough to keep earrings in, or letters. The asking price was three dollars. I didn't know enough to bargain, so I offered the woman full price and walked away from the booth with my new treasure.

The box should have rested on four Scrabble tile-sized

blocks, but one was missing. It teetered slightly on a hard surface. Bruce offered to find a piece of wood and fix it for me. When we arrived back at Tom's parents' house, his mother suggested adding some fabric to the inside.

She said, "Just find a remnant of something—velvet, maybe —and glue it in. Should be easy."

"Sure, I could do that." I sewed many of my clothes all through high school, and this wasn't even a sewing project. I liked the idea.

When Bruce and I got home, I looked for some fabric to put inside the box. I found some burgundy velvet and bought a small piece of it. The fabric cost more than the box had. Once I'd cut the velvet and glued it inside, and the little square of wood was affixed for balance, the box was complete and better than new. I kept special jewelry in it for years, until I needed more space and got a bigger box as a gift from Bruce.

I remember what was in that little cedar box. It was an embroidery sampler that my sister made when she was eight and I was six. During the year we lived in New York while my father worked on his doctorate, a neighbor taught my sister how to make several kinds of stitches and knots. On a hemmed oval of white cotton, my sister had chain-stitched R I S A in red, inside a border of blue cross-stitching. Simple pink and yellow daisies dotted with French knots were embroidered around the letters in random fashion. That sampler had survived my childhood, adolescence, early years of marriage, and a number of moves. I can still see it in my mind's eye: a sweet reminder of when her small hands labored to make me something special, with my name on it.

PINK-AND-WHITE BOX

THE CARDBOARD BOX I KEPT ON THE TOP SHELF OF MY closet held precious letters and poems and other mementos of my life before I got married. Pink and white flowers were printed all over it. The box originally held several new pairs of nylon stockings. Inside were:

- Several letters from my Grampa Mike, written in his beautiful flowing longhand on onionskin paper, in English—with a little Polish and Yiddish thrown in. The ones I remember are those in which he gushed about my letters to him. He loved getting letters from me and always urged me to write more.

- A birthday card from an older family friend, a retired librarian, to whom I had confided my eagerness to grow up and live my own life when I was still a teenager. One year she had included this poem by Edna St. Vincent Millay:

  "Was it for this I uttered prayers,
  And sobbed and cursed and kicked the stairs,
  That now, domestic as a plate, I should retire at half-past eight?"

- An envelope that contained a blank piece of paper, folded around several brilliant autumn leaves in hues of orange and yellow and red, sent from a friend at an East Coast college.

- Beautifully written poems written aboard a Coast Guard ship anchored off the coast of Alaska, composed by the boy who had broken my heart when I was seventeen. Some of his artwork was in the box also. He died young, at twenty-six, and these were the only things I had to remember him by. No one else had ever seen them.

METAL BOX

A SMALL METAL BOX IN THE GARAGE HELD THE photographs taken during Caitlin's birth. A nurse had grabbed the camera from Bruce as I was in the final stages of labor, catching on film the moment the baby's head crowned and her gradual emergence into the world. There were a few pictures of Bruce in his red-and-blue-striped T-shirt with the white collar, holding the bundle of baby and beaming at her. Two of the less graphic pictures are in one of our photo albums: me holding a very serious-looking infant in my arms, and Bruce looking exhausted and exhilarated at the same time. Hours later, he would be riding off with her in an ambulance, leaving me alone to wonder what was wrong and when or if I would ever see her again.

DRESS BOX

A LARGE BROWN BOX ON A SHELF IN THE GARAGE HELD my wedding dress, the wreath I'd worn in my hair, and the lace fan I carried when we got married in 1973, when I was twenty-one. I made my own dress in the hippie style of the day: long and flowing with an empire waist, gathered sleeves with a ruffled cuff, deep ruffle at the hem, lace trim around the square neckline and the seam that joined the bodice to the skirt.

The dress was made of pink embroidered cotton with an overlay of ecru chiffon. I wanted to create a pale shade of pink, and the combined fabrics gave me just the effect I wanted. I remember going to the fabric store with my parents to select the fabric and having an argument with my mother about it. My dad intervened and lobbied on my behalf. The wreath was my idea: baby's breath and pale pink roses. My mother suggested the fan—pink, with roses at the base and a ribbon that trailed down—instead of a bouquet.

The flowers on the wreath and fan had faded and dried out long ago, but the dress and the fan were still the same color when I peeked in the box during the move to Hermosa. It wasn't the type of thing I would have passed along to my daughter, but you just don't throw out a wedding dress.

Several years after the fire, on a visit to the Frick Collection in New York, I happened upon a portrait by James Abbott McNeill Whistler. The seven-foot-tall portrait is called "Symphony in Flesh Color and Pink: Portrait of Mrs. Frances Leyland." She is posed in such a way that we see her from the back, with her head in profile. Her long, flowing dress is the same color as my wedding dress—a combination of the same two colors to make that shade of pink—with flowers embroidered on the hem. Struck by the similarity, I bought a print of the painting and had it framed. The print now hangs in the room where I write.

LOVE LETTERS IN A BOX

I SAVED EVERY LETTER BRUCE WROTE TO ME, FROM THE first message on a long roll of Zig-Zag papers containing the words to "Both Sides Now" by Joni Mitchell, to the letters he wrote from summer camp after we graduated from high school, to the ones he sent during his first year away at college. They were all stuffed in a brown cardboard box. After that first year, he'd moved back home, which meant that our correspondence declined. He had saved my letters to him too, in a separate box. Both boxes were tucked away in a cupboard in the garage. Neither of us thought to grab them.

I used to worry about our kids discovering the letters someday, wondering how they would react to seeing (and reading, probably) the stack of letters we wrote each other when we were teenagers. There was no need to worry about that after the fire.

My parents saved their letters to each other from when they were first married, during the times they were apart to visit family in the Midwest, or when my father was in New York taking classes toward earning his doctorate. My parents have been gone for many years now, and my sister and I have read all their letters. Although it allowed me some insights into their relationship in those early days, I'm not sure my parents meant for anyone else to read their sometimes-steamy correspondence.

On the other hand, Bruce's handwriting is almost impossible for anyone to decipher—even me, and I've had years of practice—so even though the kids might have seen his letters someday if they hadn't burned, I doubt they could have really read them.

THE LITTLE BOX OF BUTTONS

I STARTED COLLECTING BUTTONS IN THE '60S: POLITICAL buttons, anti-war buttons, silly ones and mildly (or not so mildly obscene) ones. My aunt Ruth had a very large collection of buttons that she kept pinned to a long piece of felt on the wall in her bedroom. When I went to visit her in her Potrero Hill apartment in San Francisco, I would always inspect her button collection. She wore the appropriate button when she went on antiwar marches and when she attended demonstrations and when she stood in a picket line. She always seemed to have at least one button pinned to her jacket or hat whenever she left the house.

I copied her with my collection. I had the usual "Make Love Not War" sort of button, but I also had a few that needed explaining. When everyone was reading *Lord of the Rings*, I found buttons that were loosely translated into English as "Let the hair between your toes grow and grow," and "Welcome to Middle Earth." I had one that read simply "Belly," and one that urged the viewer to "Stop staring at my." Then there was the one that read "F*ck Censorship," which I hadn't worn in quite some time. I had a number of variations of the peace sign, my favorite being the one inside a depiction of a telephone rotary dial, a reminder of my first job with the telephone company in 1969, when I was just out of high school. You used to be able to find buttons like mine in shops all over Berkeley and San Francisco.

At Halloween a couple of years before the fire, Caitlin dressed up like a hippie. I loaned her a pair of my dangly earrings: one small ceramic disc read "LO" and the other one

"VE." She wore a peasant blouse, my purple velvet vest with silver embroidery from a shop on Telegraph Avenue in Berkeley, a pair of customized bell-bottom jeans (paisley inserts from cuff to the knee), sandals, and a carefully chosen selection of my buttons—the perfect accessories. A headband circled her naturally curly hair, and she carried a picket sign, with "Peace Now!" on one side and "Trick or Treat" on the other.

I kept my buttons in a little cardboard box inside the drawer of the secretary desk that had belonged to my grandparents. I don't remember how many I had collected over the years, but that little box was filled to the brim.

CHAPTER FOURTEEN

WE ARE THOSE OTHER PEOPLE

I t's a sad cliché: at the time of a disaster, people react the same way in front of a TV camera—teary men and women stare off at the horizon and say, "Things like this, I thought they only happened to other people." But we were those teary people, holding onto each other and asking, "Why?" In a selfish moment, I wondered why we were being tested again. Hadn't we paid our dues when our daughter was born with a heart defect? Didn't I pay those dues over the months I spent in the hospital at her side? How much bad luck can befall you in a lifetime? Can you ever feel secure once you've been on the hurting end of statistics—not once, but twice?

But you don't have time to ponder those questions when your kids see chaos all around them. They feel threatened and vulnerable. They cling to you, especially the littlest one, the kindergartener, who goes where you tell him and accepts with an eerie calm that his house burned down. And the fifth grader starts sleeping in his clothes, and you can't figure out why he does this all of a sudden, until it dawns on you that he wants to be ready in case there's a fire in the middle of the night. And the oldest is determined to break all the established rules—I can eat in my room, I can watch all the TV I want to, I can boss my brothers, have boys over when no one else is home because everything is different.

And we're tired, Bruce and I. Tired of being the grown-ups, tired of being responsible, tired of reminding, tired of trying to answer the questions for which there are no answers. We're tired, and yet we can't rest, can't stop, can't keep looking back and asking what if and why. We're tired, but we hang on to each other. We are surrounded by loving friends and family members, and yet we are alone too. When the friends leave and the casseroles stop coming, we're still here, still coping with each day's challenges.

WE FACED AN ENORMOUS RESPONSIBILITY: TO MAKE THE unsettled feel like normal, to pull together those loose threads and weave them into a life for our kids. Were we capable?

I had never felt the burden of being a responsible parent the way I did in the weeks and months after the fire. I still had a job, working as a counselor to parents with critically ill and premature newborns. So at a time when I doubted my own capability to find equilibrium in my new circumstances, I had to present an aura of calm and offer support to people who were feeling distraught. I'm not sure now how I did it, or if I did it well in spite of everything. I didn't want to let anyone down, but I was running on empty a lot of the time.

—————— ARTIFACT ——————

🔥

RED CHINA

WHEN WE GOT ENGAGED AND STARTED PLANNING OUR
wedding, people asked us if we had registered anywhere. We
were decidedly not into things like that, preferring to keep the
whole wedding thing low-key and stress-free. We were only
twenty-one and didn't know the first thing about the intri-
cacies of getting married. We were friends with one married
couple, but they had eloped and were borderline hippies like
us. No department store registry, we decided. Too mainstream
and establishment. Plus, Bruce hated to shop, and I knew he
would never consent to being dragged through Macy's
houseware department to look at stuff.

But we eventually succumbed to parental pressure and
decided that since we liked to cook together, it would be nice
to have a complete set of dishes instead of the mismatched
hand-me-downs we would be combining when we got married. There used to be a lovely store in Berkeley called Fraser's
that sold unique household items like furniture, dishes,
flatware, and jewelry. It was my favorite place to look around
on my lunch hour when I worked and attended classes on the
Berkeley campus. I counted on finding something there that
would mollify the parents and fill a need to our liking.

The moment we saw the red china at Fraser's, we knew
we'd found what we wanted: Thomas Flame. The bright red

plates were rimmed with black—simple, dramatic, a statement that said, "Yes, we registered for china, but we did it our way." We registered for large and small plates, bowls, cups and saucers, cream pitcher and sugar bowl, and one platter.

Our wedding guests were generous. We received eight place settings. Several of the large plates got chipped over the years, but we still had everything we'd received as wedding gifts. The Thomas Flame pattern was new the year we got married—1973—and was discontinued in 1996. Fraser's went out of business a very long time ago.

We didn't use our wedding china very often once we had a family, but every now and again, on a Friday night when the kids were in bed, we'd have a nice dinner and use those beautiful red plates.

ARTIFACT

■

MY BLUE GLOVE

MY DAD TAUGHT MY SISTER AND ME HOW TO PLAY baseball in our backyard, using a tree branch and a tennis ball. I'm not sure why he never bought us a bat and a real ball, but we managed to break the neighbor's window anyhow. I was pitching and had just pissed my sister off somehow, so she really slugged it hard.

We both played with the boys at recess, and I loved it. As a lefty, I usually hit the ball between first and second, and on rare occasions hit high fly balls to right field.

BRUCE GAVE ME THE PEACOCK-BLUE GLOVE FOR MY birthday when I was nineteen. We used to play pick-up games of softball on the weekends with friends from high school and college. We were never sure who would show up, and who would bring the beer. The only picture I have of that glove is, unfortunately, in black and white—taken at a surprise twentieth birthday party for Bruce at Live Oak Park in Berkeley.

During the late '60s through the '70s, the Oakland A's had two pitchers on the roster with "blue" in their names: Vida Blue, and Blue Moon Odom. My blue glove had Vida's name in it, since he was a southpaw like me. I took my glove to every game because there were never any extra left-handed ones to borrow.

Years later, from 1980 to 1984, when we lived on Florence Avenue in Oakland, I discovered a group of women who liked to play softball. Our season spanned the summer months, and we assembled at the local parochial school's diamond on Tuesday evenings. By then, my glove—much loved and well used—began to lose some of its vibrant blueness and showed some wear in the pocket.

We rarely had enough women to field two full teams, so we started inviting the oldest kids to join in our games. One family had ten terrific kids, and they had nice friends, so we were seldom short-handed after that. If we were desperate, we might invite a husband or two to play, but it changed the climate of the game: they would tell us to "choke up" before they'd even seen us swing the bat; they crowded in front of us when a fly ball came our way, and they offered unsolicited advice about field position. We liked it better when it was just moms and kids playing.

I joked with the group that I'd planned my third pregnancy for the off-season. As soon as I was able, I was back in the game, with nursing breaks between innings.

On Labor Day, we'd arrange a huge potluck to celebrate the end of the season. All the families showed up, and it was a wonderful way to wrap up so many summer nights of noncompetitive fun.

Eventually, the older kids went off to college or got jobs and lost interest in playing. Some of us moved away. I missed those summer evening games.

BRUCE BOUGHT ME A NEW GLOVE AFTER THE FIRE, BUT I rarely used it. We may have played a few games of catch with the kids before they grew older and lost interest too. The replacement glove wasn't blue, and it never felt right on my hand.

It takes time to break in a new glove; the new one remains stiff and unyielding, gathering cobwebs on a shelf in the garage.

CHAPTER FIFTEEN

———————

OTHER PEOPLE'S STORIES

No Room in the Trunk

Chris, my neighbor, told me that her husband filled the trunk of their car with his two accordions and his lute. This didn't leave much room for anything else. This is the same husband who thought to grab Chris's shoes and her strapless bra, but no family pictures.

Picnic

Some well-meaning friends stopped by Chris's house and thought they could eat the sandwiches they'd brought while they all watched the fire. No one knew yet how bad it would get. The sandwiches were left behind.

The Dog

Chris opened gates up and down the block so the animals could get out.

But the guy who lived next door to her was out that day.

He'd left his dog at home. Chris says she would have broken in if she'd known the dog was there. When her neighbor was allowed back into his house, he found the dog's skeleton inside.

BLIND TASTING

A guy somewhere in the neighborhood was a big wine collector. He had quite a cellar, with vintage wines and the kinds of bottles you save for special occasions. He also had a swimming pool in his backyard. He saw the fire approaching and figured he could save his wine collection if he tossed the bottles in the pool, which he did before he evacuated. When he came back to see what happened to his house, he found his wine bottles, still intact, floating around in the pool. Except all the labels had come off. He drank mystery wine for a long time.

SMELLS LIKE DRESDEN

A friend told Bruce this story: He'd met a guy who'd moved to the Oakland Hills from Germany a number of years before the fire. He had been in Dresden when it was bombed in WWII. The guy's house in the hills was destroyed by the fire. When he went to see what was left of it, he said, "It smells like Dresden here."

I LEFT MY FIDDLE

My friend Sara was home with her seven-year-old daughter Jenny on Sunday, the day of the fire. Her husband, John, was on a sailboat on the bay with a friend. He told her later he could see the smoke from the boat.

Sara stayed home until late in the afternoon. At first police told folks to stay put. Later, they drove around the neighborhood and ordered people to evacuate.

Chris, Sara, and I all lived on the same block, across the street from the elementary school our children attended. After Chris and I evacuated, the school principal somehow drove through the fire from her home in Walnut Creek and opened the classroom doors. She went from room to room, bringing out the guinea pigs and the pet snake, handing them off to neighbors and putting some of them in her own car.

Sara and John connected by phone when he got back on land, and they had a quick conversation about what she should take with her. John's woodworking tools—essential to his livelihood as a cabinetmaker and carpenter—filled their garage. Sara had a fiddle she loved to play. She'd had it for many years. But she didn't take any of his tools or her beautiful fiddle. Her family pictures were scattered around the house and not easily gathered up.

"Just get yourselves out of there," John had said. Sara didn't have a cat carrier, so she scooped the family cat into a pillowcase and drove with Jenny to meet John down at the waterfront in Berkeley. They had agreed to meet at a roadside café they didn't know the name of, but they found each other anyway.

She figured everything would burn, judging from the speed of the approaching flames at the time she left the block. But it didn't. Her house survived, one of two on our block left standing.

Everything in her backyard burned, but the fire stopped short of the house.

We talked recently about that Sunday, and she told me something I hadn't heard before: the new pearl earrings she'd just bought and left on her bedside table, once a creamy white, had changed color. They took on the color of smoke, she said.

Did she feel lucky? She says no. The day-to-day horror of living there surrounded by destruction, followed by the day-to-day nuisance of massive construction is something she will never forget. Coming back to live on our block after the fire was miserably lonely and, once construction began, dusty and noisy. She pointed out that we don't hear too much about the people who evacuated and came back to find their houses standing in the middle of a moonscape. And the fire was so random: one house burned, the rest of the block remained intact —or the reverse. The pattern varied from block to block, mystifying both those who felt fortunate and those who didn't.

Sometime after the fire, Sara spoke to another neighbor who mentioned in passing that God's will had something to do with why his house was spared while others burned. She never spoke to that neighbor again. I'm glad she never told me who it was.

WHAT CINDY SAW

My friend and around-the-corner neighbor, Cindy, was at the Oakland Zoo with her family on Sunday at around noon. She noticed what she thought were small grey insects on her black shirt. And then a woman standing nearby guessed that they were bits of ash from the fire in the hills.

Cindy was overcome with guilt: she'd left a partially thawed turkey, with the package of gizzards still inside, cooking at home. She was certain that it was her oven—her turkey—that caused the fire.

Racing home on the highway, she heard the sirens and saw the billowing black smoke above the hills to the east of her house and realized that the fire couldn't have started with her turkey after all.

Once she got home, she heard news of the fire spreading rapidly among the neighbors: the fire had jumped the freeways; people were running for their lives.

A friend came by and offered to take Cindy's kids—seven and five years old—to a safe place out of the area. The kids left and stayed away for several days with the friend's family.

Cindy and her husband got busy: they packed up furniture and rugs, and brought them over to our friend Janiele's house in Piedmont; they made seven trips in all. In the early evening, the wind changed and the air cooled a bit, down from the ninety-two-degree heat of the afternoon. She could still hear helicopters and sirens, and a new sound: abandoned cars exploding as the fire consumed them.

She'd been watching the news and the fire at the same time. The picture on her TV mirrored what was going on overhead: smoke, ash, helicopters, flying embers. When the fire came over the hill, it was "a hot curtain of orange." She says she could feel the full heat of it on her face, that her skin felt dry and chapped.

When the power went out around 7:15, she and her husband decided it was time to leave. They saw downed power lines "spitting sparks" as they evacuated.

Cindy saw my house and John and Chris's house burn. She

described how it looked: the front windows blown out, curtains blazing.

A state trooper told her later that if she'd waited ten more minutes to leave, she would not have been able to drive out of the neighborhood.

Her husband snuck back in around midnight. He learned that, thanks to their next-door neighbor who'd defied orders to evacuate, their house was still standing. The neighbor had sat on his roof all night with a running hose, dousing embers as they flew and landed on their roofs and on his just-finished $50,000 deck. His house didn't burn.

A neighbor of ours did the same thing: stayed behind with a hose to protect the house he'd been building for the last six years. His house—with a redwood exterior—did not burn either. I heard later that he risked his life by staying, but he said he would have gone down with the house.

I have never for one second regretted leaving when we did. I don't think our house could have been saved. I learned later from Cindy how the firefighters had made a stand in the street in front of my house to save the neighborhood schools, and I couldn't fault them for that.

Cindy remembers coming back to the neighborhood with a police escort two days later and seeing the black expanse all the way up the hills, the burnt remnants of cars left on the street, and all the chimneys.

WE MADE IT THROUGH, THANK GOD

This story is told by Dwight Langford, an Oakland fire investigator called in for active firefighting duty. The interview was published in *The Express*, a local paper, a few days after the fire.

He was near the source of the fire, on Marlborough Terrace, and saw it grow from a small brush fire to an uncontrollable blaze. He was trapped by the flames:

"We were on the scene all night and all morning. Suddenly the fire changed directions. It came up the canyon in minutes. There were three of us and only one road in. We tried to go around but the fire blocked us in, it surrounded us. We prepared for what was to come. I saw everything I ever did flash in front of my eyes. We just sat there for an hour, wetting each other down. At its worst we were a couple of feet from the flames, with nowhere to go. My helmet melted. We saw it coming, but there wasn't a whole lot we could do. We would have had to be supermen to get out of there. Suddenly the wind changed and the fire changed directions, and we were able to get out. We made it through, thank God."

I Decided I Had to Live

A year or so after the fire, I had lunch in Oakland with a new friend who was involved in the same kind of counseling work I did. We talked about our jobs and so on, and, as it inevitably did—and still does—the subject of the fire came up.

"Were you burned out?" she asked me.

I said yes, and then I gave her the practiced version of my experience.

"And what about you?" I asked. She paused a moment and then told me where she'd been during the fire.

She'd been swimming in a pool up near Hiller Highlands,

close to where the fire started. She and another woman were changing out of their suits and missed the warnings to evacuate. They stepped outside and saw that the fire was coming right at them. The two women grabbed towels and jumped back in the pool. They stayed under water as the fire swept over them, coming up for air when their lungs screamed out. They kept the towels over their heads to keep the hot ashes from scorching their scalps. Under and up, breathe; under and up, breathe—over and over in the water until the fire passed over them. When my friend was in the water, ducking flames and ash, she told herself that she had to stay alive for her daughter's sake, and she believes that this is the only thing that saved her.

She showed me her car keys. The keys were fine, but the metal holder was twisted out of shape. That's what the fire did, she said. By some miracle, her car was untouched, so as soon as she could, she got herself and the other woman out of the water and away from further danger.

I could not begin to imagine what that must have felt like: ducking under water as the fire swept over her head, knowing that she had to make it home so she could hold her precious daughter in her arms once more.

—————————— ARTIFACT ——————————

🔥

AUNT AUGUSTA'S CHAIR

I FIRST SAW THIS CHAIR IN THE CORNER OF MY THEN-boyfriend's bedroom in 1968—piled high with clothes, its upholstery faded and tattered, its walnut arms and legs black with grime. I asked him about the chair, which was an odd accompaniment to his Fillmore concert posters and hi-fi equipment. "Oh, that's Aunt Augusta's chair," he told me. Some old great-aunt of his father's who'd been dead for decades. The chair had seen much better days, I'd guessed, but there was something about it I liked; it had a certain dignity to it, despite its derelict appearance.

When the boyfriend and I got married, Aunt Augusta's chair came with us. Once we removed the grime from the wood and had the fabric replaced, the chair regained its former bearing. The carvings on the legs and the flocked floral upholstery revealed the noble qualities that had been there all along. Because of our cats' sharp claws, however, the chair required a subsequent makeover several years later. Augusta's chair moved with us from our one-bedroom apartment in Albany to our rental house in San Jose, back to the Bay Area, to two more rentals, and finally to the blue house on Hermosa Avenue in Oakland. The chair got one final makeover: in a light-blue pattern to match the fabric on our dining room chairs.

Aunt Augusta's chair features prominently in family photographs. We're holding the baby in one house; the big sister holds her baby brother in another; the three kids gather around in funny hats or party clothes in the living room of our blue house. Pictures of a family growing up fill the albums we took with us, and that chair is always in the background.

———————— ARTIFACT ————————

♨

THE SECRETARY DESK

MY GRAMPA MIKE WAS A MISGUIDED BUSINESSMAN. THE
stories about his failed or ill-conceived business ventures are
legendary in my father's family. My grandfather, born Morris
(or Moses), became Mike when he opened a bar in San
Francisco's Skid Row in the 1940s. After the bar, he got into
the egg business in Petaluma, like many of his countrymen from
Russia who immigrated to California. But instead of trying to
raise chickens, he became an egg wholesaler, supplying eggs to
restaurants and bars in the city. After he sold the bar, he tried a
number of other businesses, including hotel management. He
bought a couple of motels in Northern California, one with
rooms that rented by the hour—something he was unaware of
at the time he bought it.

Based on the kind of person my grandfather was, I'm sure
his record-keeping was sketchy at best. For as long as I'd known
him, the wooden desk—piled high with receipts, invoices, and
scraps of paper—leaned against the wall in the back room of his
San Francisco apartment. This piece of furniture would be
more accurately described as a secretary desk, since it had a
hinged section that folded down to a ninety-degree angle, forming a writing surface. But my grandfather's desk was always
open, revealing the inside compartments that were stuffed with
papers. A little drawer separated the vertical dividers, and

underneath both there was more space to cram papers and envelopes. The secretary had clawed feet and carved legs, which you would hardly notice because of the cluttered surfaces and interior.

Some months after my grandfather died, I mentioned the desk to my Grandma Eve. I said, "That's the only thing of Grampa's that I would really like to have."

She replied, "Actually, it's mine." Oh. I hadn't realized that. She had married my grandfather after his first wife passed away. He employed the services of a matchmaker who fixed him up with Eve. She must have shipped her desk and other belongings to San Francisco when she moved out from Cleveland to get married. I never considered that the secretary might have been hers. But she didn't seem to mind that I staked a claim on it.

SEVERAL YEARS LATER, MY AUNTS, MY SISTER, AND I HAD the task of clearing out my grandparents' apartment after Eve died. Among other remnants of their life together, we found many unfinished knitting projects, a box full of men's combs with one of my grandfather's ill-fated business names on them, and a mysterious black velvet dress.

No one objected when I mentioned that I wanted to take the secretary. I was amazed to discover the intricate pattern that lay hidden on the underside (actually, the outside) of the hinged section of the desk. When the horizontal piece was lifted up and snapped closed, the desk looked stately and elegant. I brought it home, cleaned and polished it, replaced some of the hardware, and stood back to admire its rich, deep walnut color. This was a far cry from the cluttered dumping ground it had been for years at my grandparents' apartment. The desk appears in countless family pictures, the top covered with family photos. We gave it the second life it deserved.

PART 3

CHAPTER SIXTEEN

HOME AGAIN

January 29, 1993

After nine months of construction, things were close enough to being done that we were able to move in. Even though the painters were doing touchups and other workmen were still around, we'd packed up and moved all the things we'd managed to accumulate since the fire into the new, almost-ready house.

The day began with our last morning drive from Moraga, during which Caitlin read out loud from *Winnie the Pooh*. Everyone got bagels for lunch, then I dropped them off at school.

We told the boys they could walk home after school, across the street to the new house.

When the bell rang at 3:00 that afternoon they ran up the block and stood on the front porch, hopping with excitement. I opened the door, and they came inside. "We're home! We're finally home!" they said, and I caught the contractors wiping away tears.

That first night in the new house the wind blew fiercely
and kept us awake. We left on a windy day . . . full circle. But
it was good to be home, at last.

IN PREPARING FOR OUR FIRST THANKSGIVING BACK IN
the new house, we kept going to closets that weren't there
anymore to look for stuff we no longer had. That big white
tablecloth? Prefire. Gravy boat? Nope. Platter for the turkey?
Isn't it in the . . . ? Nope. Where are the big knives? Wait . . .

we don't have any. After a while, we just assumed that stuff we were sure we had was no longer in the house, the attic, the garage, any closet . . . it only existed in our memories. It got to be a joke. But in the end, stuff can be replaced, which is why we now own at least three gravy ladles. Every once in a while, I go looking for something—one of those once-a-year things—and then I remember. Still, after twenty-five years.

THE BRILLIANT-YELLOW DAFFODILS CAME BACK THAT FIRST February after the fire, right where they'd been before. Despite everything, they poked through the ashes and the dirt and stood tall, nodding their heads in welcome.

CHAPTER SEVENTEEN

MY JOURNAL

I kept a journal during the months of construction, a chronicle of the everyday and the extraordinary: a showdown with a contractor; a note about James's letter to the tooth fairy, reminding her he'd lost two teeth this time; complications and angry tears because of rain delays interspersed with election news: my son lost his bid to be student body president and the Clintons moved into the White House. There was progress, followed by setbacks, followed by progress.

Leafing through the journal brings back those long waits, the miscommunication, the compromises, the little triumphs when work got done on time or early. I recorded every step, from the foundation to the finish work.

June 3, 1992: Demolition begins. I got to sit in the big Caterpillar and take a chunk out of the retaining wall. We took turns with a sledgehammer, knocking down the brick walls in the front.

June 5: By today, the lot looks like an empty canvas, waiting to be transformed into something very different. This is a big cut into the hill.

June 12: It's Caitlin's promotion ceremony. She wears a pink dress and carries a yellow rose. The speakers tell the kids, "These are the best years of your lives, concentrate on what's going on around you and appreciate it while it's happening now." They tell the kids, "Do what matters."

July 15: The first floor is all framed by the end of the day. While I stayed and watched, two walls went up.

July 16: We can walk around from room to room.

August 28: As of this date, the framing is done, the roof is on, the windows are in, rough plumbing has begun, and the skylights are in. It looks and feels like the house it will be. We've decided on gas, nixed stackers. I sat in the tub yesterday —it's great. The ceiling in the kitchen is also framed, and the kitchen door is in. We have stairs down to the garage and up to the second floor. The fireplace is in. We are rethinking the yard now, maybe no terraces, just a walkway.

September 13: Are we halfway there yet?

September 21: The week from hell. Bruce is traveling back East and down South, chasing luggage while I'm having a crisis of confidence over house issues. The second set of windows arrived. They're wrong also, but less wrong than the first set. What to do? The alarm company shows up unannounced and wants to know where to put stuff. And then there's the speaker-wire controversy. Help! And James has his two front teeth pulled.

September 25: Front steps and walkway to the back are poured. We have a front door now. I asked someone to take my picture knocking on the door. It feels like a real house now. The boys and I scratched our initials in wet concrete. The speaker wire issue is almost resolved. What a pain.

October 20: One year later. So hard to believe. Still no stucco. Had dinner in the new house by flashlight. Pizza on the floor, sang the hamotzi, and had a good time. James ate mushrooms in the dark, at the urging of his older brother. Many toasts. It felt good to be back. The next two months are going to be very hard.

November 3: Election Day. Bill and Al win.

November 15: A walk down College Avenue with my friends. I miss all of us living in the same neighborhood and having coffee or going on walks whenever we want.

November 16: Friends come over for a tour. There's a lock on the kitchen door now. We let ourselves in with a key.

November 24: We won't make it by Christmas. What about New Year's?

January 7, 1993: Didn't go near the place today. Everyone thinks maybe I should stay away for a while. I think they're right.

ARTIFACT

STAR-SHAPED CAKE PANS

I BOUGHT THE STAR-SHAPED CAKE PANS FROM THE BIG hardware and kitchenware store that used to be on Shattuck Avenue in Berkeley, back when Bruce and I were near the end of our senior year in high school. I knew his birthday was June 14, Flag Day, so I planned to make him a birthday cake that I would decorate with red, white, and blue icing. Making it in the shape of a star would be a surprise for him and a challenge for me. I had a well-established propensity for stars—several pairs of earrings and other accessories—so the cake pans fit right in with that leitmotif.

Then I heard that his mother was throwing a party on that particular June day in 1969—a party for herself. She had just earned her doctorate at UC Berkeley and planned a small celebration with friends and family to mark her accomplishment. It just so happened to coincide with her son's eighteenth birthday.

When I heard about the party, I was determined to make him something special to commemorate his birthday despite the ongoing hoopla for his mother. We hadn't been dating that long—only a few months—and we would soon be separated when he went away to college. I hoped to make some sort of impression with his family while not making myself too conspicuous.

I baked him a star-shaped chocolate cake and decorated it excessively with icing in the colors of the flag, with the right number of candles. I was a bit more conspicuous than I'd planned, but the cake won his heart and impressed his relatives, many of whom weren't even aware he had a girlfriend at that point.

THE FIRST YEAR WE WERE MARRIED, I MADE HIS BIRTHDAY cake from a new recipe a coworker gave me. It became my go-to cake recipe because it produced light, delicious, and chocolaty layers that rose beautifully. The chocolate buttercream frosting that accompanied the cake recipe had a hint of coffee flavor and wasn't too sweet.

For years, I would make him a Black Midnight birthday cake, baked in the shape of a star. I still have the recipe in the black binder that he carried out of the house the day of the fire.

ARTIFACT

🔥

BETTY CROCKER'S NEW
BOYS AND GIRLS COOK BOOK

I FOUND THIS CLASSIC 1950S COOKBOOK AT THE WHITE Elephant Sale—a blockbuster fundraising event held every year to benefit the Oakland Museum of California.

From the time he was old enough to look through it, James was entranced by the recipe for the Enchanted Castle Cake. This was more than just a cake; it was an architectural marvel. The castle was constructed by carefully sawing a nine-by-thirteen-inch cake (yellow, from a mix) into smaller squares, rectangles, and arches, then stacking and arranging the pieces, applying frosting (also from a mix), and decorating the whole affair with marshmallows, chocolate, inverted ice cream cones, and toothpicks to create an impressive castle with flags, turrets, and a drawbridge.

James really, really wanted to make that castle cake, but there was always something more pressing to do. Promises were made to make it, but that day never came.

Although my husband thought to rescue our big binder of handwritten recipes when he left the house on the day of the fire, the *Boys and Girls Cook Book* was left behind.

I don't think I understood how much James missed this book until he started talking about the castle cake again. How would I ever find a copy of this book, long out of print?

A neighbor whose house didn't burn made it her job to help the rest of us replace our favorite cookbooks. She asked us for a list of books we would want to replace, then she set to work, using her publishing connections.

To those of us starting all over, having our favorite recipes again allowed us to start putting our lives back together. In an unfamiliar rental house, an unfamiliar neighborhood, and a different kitchen, being able to cook family favorites was a blessing.

Months passed, and I had given up trying to replace my vintage Betty Crocker cookbook. But then Paula, the neighbor with foodie connections, put me in touch with a man from General Mills, Betty Crocker's parent company. We talked about the *Boys and Girls Cook Book*, and I explained my six-year-old son's fascination with the Enchanted Castle Cake. Oh yes, he was familiar with the castle cake. Yes, he had a copy of the cookbook. No, I couldn't have it. But he offered to make a copy of the recipe and illustrations and send it to me, which he did, and hope was restored in James's heart.

I confess I didn't jump right up and bake the cake. It was still a huge hassle, and besides, I didn't have anything to bake with yet. It was nearly a year before I felt like baking anything.

ONE SUMMER DAY, WHEN JAMES WAS TWELVE, WE MADE the castle cake. Our cake had a definite starboard list to it, and I doubt the turrets would have survived even a minor earthquake. We took some license and liberally doused the whole structure with multicolored sprinkles. We did all of it together: placing the marshmallows like puffy luminaria atop the castle walls, frosting the upside-down ice cream cones, creating waves of blue icing (for the moat), placing jaunty little paper flags into the tops of the tilted towers—the whole shebang. Our special touch: chocolate dorsal fins placed menacingly in the moat.

I took several pictures, for it was a sight to behold. If, after all those years, it didn't meet his expectations, James never let on.

WHEN JAMES WAS A SENIOR IN HIGH SCHOOL, GETTING ready to fill out his college applications, I asked him what he would write his personal statement about. He said, "The castle cake."

"Really?" I asked him.

"Maybe," he said.

He eventually chose to write about something else, but it brought back some happy memories of the day we made that cake together. I did write about it, however, and my essay was published in the *San Francisco Chronicle*'s Sunday magazine— my first big-deal local publication.

I was dumbfounded at the number of letters I received in response to my essay. Apparently a lot of people owned that cookbook as children, and some had even made the Enchanted Castle Cake.

But the best part of all was when Joan, a writer friend whose children were grown up and on their own, gave me her well-loved copy of the cookbook.

I still have it.

CHAPTER EIGHTEEN

DRAWING FROM THE FIRE

Several months after the fire, a graduate student from Stanford made a short film about the children of Hillcrest School, called *Drawing from the Fire*. He spent time in the classroom and interviewed a number of fifth graders and their families. The school district brought in counselors to help start discussions about what had happened and how the kids reacted. One of the ways the counselors got kids to talk was to encourage them to draw pictures of what they saw and how they felt.

Myles was one of the kids featured in this film, and I obtained a copy of it. Never one to hold back on expressing himself, Myles was very articulate about his visceral response on the day of the fire. He was asked to draw a picture of himself and explain it to the other kids in the group.

In his words, describing his self-portrait: "My feet had million-pound weights on them. I found it hard to move. It was like I was underwater, like in a dream. It was very difficult. My knees registered a ten on the Richter scale. I couldn't stand still [and felt] kind of wobbly. Someone was riding a bike in my stomach. I felt queasy. There was a pounding bell in my heart: thump, thump, thump. My eyes and nose were running nonstop. I was really scared and worried."

At the end of the film, the interviewer used clips from Myles and me. We were seated in the living room of our rental house in Moraga. I spoke in a very measured, unemotional tone about all the help parents got from the school and from other parents who reached out and formed a buddy system to bring us food or watch our kids or pick them up from school.

But the final lines are from Myles, spoken over a haunting piece of music: "It's important that people don't forget this, because it could happen again next week. People are saying, if there's another fire, we may not be able to rebuild . . . so you get closer to your friends, you spend a lot more time with the people you love . . . and it's good. You learn something from what's happened to you."

———————— ARTIFACT ————————

🔥

THE INDOOR NOISY BOOK

THE INDOOR NOISY BOOK, BY MARGARET WISE BROWN, was written in 1942. This little book was a birthday gift from my across-the-street neighbor John on my fourth or fifth birthday. We were frequent playmates, and he is there in all my birthday party pictures: a small strawberry blond who stands shyly off to the side.

The book was inscribed to me. He had written: "To Risa from John" inside with a crayon, but the slanted leg on the R was doing a high kick and the S was backwards.

I brought that book with me when I moved out of my parents' house. It survived several moves after that as well: to Berkeley, Oakland, back to Berkeley, Albany, San Jose, and back to Oakland after Caitlin was born.

I READ THIS LITTLE BOOK TO MY THREE CHILDREN, WHO will invariably say, "The little dog Muffin has a cold," when they are sick—even now that they are all grown up. (Muffin is the main character in this story and must stay inside all day to rest.) The line is part of the family lexicon.

This sweet little book with its bold colors and stylized illustrations was one of my most prized possessions—one of only two physical remnants of my early childhood.

SEVERAL YEARS AGO, CAITLIN MANAGED TO LOCATE A COPY of the book on eBay and surprised me with it on Christmas. I laughed, I cried, I read it out loud.

A treasured link to my childhood, and to those of my children, was given back to me. I never dreamed I'd have that book again. It was one of the best gifts I ever received.

THERE WAS A FIRE HERE

October 20, 1991. Oakland, California

There was a fire here. It started high above our house, on a hill facing west. No one knows for certain how it started, but a human hand set something burning and started the fire. The fire incinerated, it eliminated; it scorched, it singed; it destroyed, it killed. The fire sent black smoke miles into the sky, sent clouds of ash floating west to the sea. It created its own weather.

There was a fire here. It started on a Saturday afternoon in October, a day of college football in nearby Berkeley, where leaves in brilliant shades of orange and red fluttered to the sidewalks under a clear sky. On Saturday, we didn't smell smoke, didn't feel a hot wind blowing. But we heard the helicopters buzzing overhead, saw their propellers slicing the air. From their bellies, buckets swung on wire cables like pendulums, sloshing water as they flew, on their way to fight the blaze. The fire chief spoke on TV that Saturday evening; he reported that the fire was out. The sparks and embers had been extinguished. A disaster averted. Thank God. No fire.

But the next day, in the early hours of that warm Sunday morning, a northeasterly wind, an unseasonable force, fanned the dying embers, blew them hot into the air, to the tops of the eucalyptus trees and into the desiccated high brush covering the autumn-brown hills above our houses and spread the flames. A hot, dry wind blowing from the wrong direction, a demonic force, the devil's breath you cannot see makes trees sway, sparks fly, and embers leap from treetop to treetop, bringing heat and fire; and the fire, snapping like a fingernail on a match head, raged through anything in its path—anything at all. Everything.

The fire leveled homes to their concrete foundations. It killed a teacher, a student, a grandmother, a fire battalion chief, a police officer; twenty-five men and women, young and old. It took the lives of dogs and cats trapped in their houses. It charred the habitats of deer, raccoon, skunk, and possum. The mocking bird that serenaded from morning trees outside my window, hummingbirds with red throats that sipped from the flowers in my garden, the yellow finches, black crows, and brown sparrows—all left homeless, with no eaves or branches for their nests. The fire destroyed the liquidambar tree in front of my house, the one that marked the seasons with its spring green, its fall orange, its winter black.

It robbed us of heirlooms and wedding presents, works of art, novels in progress, a lifetime of photographs; first-place trophies and blue ribbons, seashells and stuffed animals, secrets tucked away in boxes and under beds; letters, diplomas, year-books, dolls, toy trucks, baseballs, crayons, bicycles, and report cards; blankets and pillows, mattresses and cribs, storybooks and night-lights, shoes, and sweaters. It turned everything into ash and left the twisted metal skeletons of bed frames.

There was a fire here that firefighters couldn't beat. It raced down narrow, crooked streets, outrunning people, animals, and cars. No time to get out, no time to go back, no time to think. Firefighters rushed from far away, only to stand by, watching, helpless, holding hoses that didn't fit hydrants—hoses rendered useless. Smoke filled their lungs, soot blackened their faces. The fire pressed them back, winds gusting, roaring and ripping over the trees and roofs; trees exploding into sparks and flames, roofs catching the sparks from trees, wooden shingles feeding the flames, windows bursting, shattered glass flying, houses collapsing onto themselves, imploding one floor, then another, then another, until they piled on their foundations like smashed layer cakes—splintered, ruined, unrecognizable. The extreme heat freed dormant seeds, waiting for decades for fire to set them loose from the trees. And blackened scarecrows were left to watch over a lonely landscape.

The fire jumped across eight lanes of one freeway and four lanes of another, careering down the hills, leaving nothing standing except red brick chimneys, garden walls, and steadfast barbecues meant to hold fire inside them. In the aftermath, a hardened swath of vile black stretched in all directions; hot sulfuric fumes permeated the air. Gone: our blue house, our pink roses, our wooden fences, our children's tree house, our white front door. It is gone, beyond my concept of gone.

There was a fire here that wiped out not only things, not only people, but memories—a past with nothing left to mark its presence. The fire erased the acquisitions of a life together: a widow's keepsakes, faded corsages and pressed bouquets. Holocaust survivors lost everything, again. Children lost neighbors who handed them candy on Halloween and delivered cookies at Christmas, who left Easter baskets on the doorstep and invited everyone up on the deck to watch fireworks on the Fourth of July.

There was a fire. And then there was everything that happened after. When the fire stopped burning, when the rains came, when police removed the yellow-tape barriers, when the neighbors returned to the death and destruction, we held onto each other and tried not to ask why, tried not to wonder what next, tried to imagine starting over.

There was a fire here that tore some families apart and pulled others closer together. Couples argued and blamed each other for leaving belongings behind. Marriages unraveled. Children accused their parents of allowing their homes to burn; they got angry when they learned there wasn't a bad guy to catch and put in jail for starting the fire. People wrangled with authorities and insurance companies over the value of their property and the contents of their houses. Some found that they didn't have enough insurance. No one told them, or they hadn't paid attention. A curious shift occurred when the new houses went up: survivor guilt was supplanted by envy. The neighborhood became a dusty, noisy, lonely place to live, and even though it seemed like a lucky break at the time to have your house survive the fire, as the months went by and the big new houses got built, the tide turned against those who had been pitied before.

And as those new houses grew, with bigger rooms and all new things, did some of us feel the tiniest bit lucky to be starting fresh? Was being lucky part of a blessing or a curse?

There was a fire here that divided a community: survivor, victim; lucky, unlucky; before and after. If you were here then, you will remember where the lines were drawn. But as time goes by, the lines grow fainter.

THERE IS THE BEFORE, AND THEN THERE IS THE AFTER. We forget which is which sometimes, even now, even when it's been twenty-five years. We stop when we look for things. Where's that white tablecloth? Oh, yeah. . . .

There was a fire here.

APPENDIX

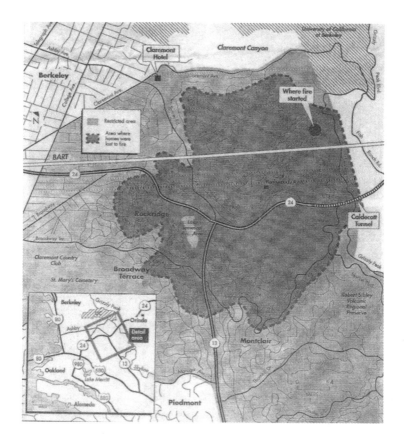

TIMELINE

Saturday, October 19

12:12 p.m. A grass fire near Grizzly peak Boulevard is reported. Fire crews quickly respond.

1:30 p.m. Fire crews report the fire is contained. Sometime later, they depart, leaving behind their equipment in case the fire rekindles. Throughout the night, firefighters patrol the area.

Sunday, October 20

8:51 a.m. Firefighters return to the fire scene to check for hot-spots and retrieve their equipment. They find smoldering grass and begin the tedious task of looking for hidden fire. The wind gets stronger.

10:53 a.m. A sudden gust of wind stirs the fire. Suddenly, flames are everywhere.

10:58 a.m. The first alarm is sounded.

11:16 a.m. The fire, now raging out of control, is classified at six-alarms. Residents flee as walls of flame rush at them.

11:45 a.m. Oakland Police Officer John Grubensky radios in. He's in trouble. His patrol car is blocked. He's trying to help residents escape the fire. It's Grubensky's last message.

12:15 p.m. Flames cut off power at EBMUD's Claremont power center, causing eight pumping plants to shut down. Water pressure drops as the inferno leapfrogs from house to house, treetop to treetop.

12:15 p.m.: The call goes out for air support. Tankers and helicopters begin dropping water.

1:15 p.m. Fire officials sound the alert for full mutual aid. Fire-fighters from across the Bay Area join with Oakland, East Bay Parks, Contra Costa and California Department of Forestry. More from other parts of the state, Oregon, and Nevada are on their way.

3:00 p.m. The streets are filled with people in panic.

3:34 p.m. Fire officials ask for four special strike teams.

6:26 p.m. The sun sets on the inferno, still blazing out of control.

Excerpted from *The Contra Costa Times* Special Report

IN MEMORY OF:

Eunice Barkell, 79. Found in her house on Charing Cross Road.

Gail Baxter, 61. Found in the road on Charing Cross Road.

May Elizabeth Blos, 85. Found on Live Oak Road.

Mary Lucile Brantly, 78. Found in her home on Binnacle Hill Road.

Robert Emery Cox, 64. Found with Terry DuPont, in backyard on Chancellor Place.

Terry DuPont, 58. Found with Robert Emery Cox.

Carolyn Grant, 75. Found in remains of house on Marlin Cove Road.

John Alexander Grant, 77. Found with his wife Carolyn, in their house.

John Grubensky, 32. Found on Charing Cross Road, near Gail Baxter and Phillip Loggins.

Segall Livnah, 18. Found in street midblock on Windward Hill.

Phillip Loggins, 51. Found on Charing Cross Road near John Grubensky and Gail Baxter.

Lucy Chi-Win Mantz, 46. Found in remains of house on Schooner Hill Road.

Gregor McGinnis, 46. Found in backyard of house on Bristol Drive.

Lewis D. McNeary, Jr., 44. Found on Charing Cross Road.

Patrick Emmett O'Neill, 40. Found on Bristol Drive.

Leigh Ortenberger, 62. Found in driveway of house on Charing Cross Road.

James Riley, 49. Found on Norfolk Road next to Kimberly Robson.

Kimberly Robson, 37. Found in driveway next to James Riley on Norfolk Road.

Francis Gray Scott, 37. Found in house on Alvarado Road.

Virginia P. Smith, 61. Found in driveway on Charing Cross Road.

Anne Tagore, 54. Found in house on Norfolk Road.

Aina Turjanis, 64. Found on Charing Cross Road.

Cheryl Turjanis, 25. Found downhill from Gail Baxter on Charing Cross Road.

Paul Tryell, 61. Found in his pickup truck behind John Grubensky's patrol car on Charing Cross Road.

REFERENCES

An *Oakland Tribune* Special Edition, 2 December 1991: 74. Print.

Catania, Sara. "We Made It Through, Thank God." *Express*, Berkeley, CA, 25 October 1991: 4. Print.

Contra Costa Times Special Report, 27 October 1991: 3-7. Print.

"Fire Notebook." *Oakland Tribune*, 22 October 1991: A14. Print.

"Oakland/Berkeley Hills Fire." National Fire Protection Association in cooperation with the Oakland and Berkeley, California Fire Departments and the California State Fire Marshal's Office, 20 October 1991.

Oakes, Robert and Times wire services. "Firefighter from Martinez Among 14 Dead." *West County Times*, 22 October 1991: 1B. Print.

FEMA. "The East Bay Hills Fire." US Fire Administration/ Technical Report Series, Oakland-Berkeley, California, USFA-TR-060/October 1991. Available online at: http://www.berkeleyside.com/wp-content/uploads/2015/09/tr-060.pdf.

ACKNOWLEDGMENTS

My thanks to:

My fellow MFA nonfictionistas at Saint Mary's College who were there from the beginning;

My advisors, Marilyn Abildskov and Peter Trachtenberg, who gave me the encouragement to carry on and write this thing;

My Moms Group: friends through thick and thin for over three decades—you're in here!

The faithful Crawford Seven—past and present—for their support, patience, good humor, and sharp eyes through the many years it took for this book to take shape. A special thanks to Anne Fox for knowing where a comma belongs and where it does not;

Alex Campbell for his encouragement and good advice;

Brooke Warner for her honesty and attention, and her belief in this project;

Elizabeth Fishel and the Wednesday Writers for creating a safe place to try new things with my writing;

My sister, Susie Elkind, who is present in these pages and whose memory lives in our hearts;

To the next generation, with the hope that they will read this book some day;

And to Bruce, Caitlin, Myles, and James Nye, who graciously allowed me to tell our story here.

ABOUT THE AUTHOR

photo credit: Bruce Nye

Risa Nye is a lifelong resident of the San Francisco Bay Area. She attended the University of California, Berkeley, and earned master's degrees at both California State University East Bay and Saint Mary's College of California (MFA). Her articles and essays have appeared in a number of local and national publications, as well as in several anthologies. A coeditor of the anthology *Writin' on Empty: Parents Reveal the Upside, Downside, and Everything In Between When Children Leave the Nest,* she also recently published an e-book based on her blog, *Zero to Sixty in One Year: An Easy Month-by-Month Guide to Writing Your Life Story.* She lives in Oakland, CA, with her husband. Her writing can be found at:

www.risanye.com

SELECTED TITLES FROM SHE WRITES PRESS

She Writes Press is an independent publishing company
founded to serve women writers everywhere.
Visit us at www.shewritespress.com.

Fire Season: A Memoir by Hollye Dexter. $16.95,
978-1-63152-974-0. After she loses everything in a fire, Hollye
Dexter's life spirals downward and she begins to unravel—but
when she finds herself at the brink of losing her husband, she is
forced to dig within herself for the strength to keep her family
together.

*Renewable: One Woman's Search for Simplicity, Faithfulness, and
Hope* by Eileen Flanagan. $16.95, 978-1-63152-968-9. At age
forty-nine, Eileen Flanagan had an aching feeling that she wasn't
living up to her youthful ideals or potential, so she started trying
to change the world—and in doing so, she found the courage to
change her life.

*Where Have I Been All My Life? A Journey Toward Love and
Wholeness* by Cheryl Rice. $16.95, 978-1-63152-917-7. Rice's
universally relatable story of how her mother's sudden death
launched her on a journey into the deepest parts of grief—and,
ultimately, toward love and wholeness.

Not by Accident: Reconstructing a Careless Life by Samantha Dunn.
$16.95, 978-1-63152-832-3. After suffering a nearly fatal riding
accident, lifelong klutz Samantha Dunn felt compelled to examine
just what it was inside herself—and other people—that invited
carelessness and injury.

Four Funerals and a Wedding: Resilience in a Time of Grief by Jill
Smolowe. $16.95, 978-1-938314-72-8. When journalist Jill
Smolowe lost four family members in less than two years, she
turned to modern bereavement research for answers—and made
some surprising discoveries.

Learning to Eat Along the Way by Margaret Bendet. $16.95,
978-1-63152-997-9. After interviewing an Indian holy man,
newspaper reporter Margaret Bendet follows him in pursuit of
enlightenment and ends up facing demons that were inside her all
along.